GIANT TREES

of Western America *and* The World

GIANT TREES

of Western America *and* The World

AL CARDER

HARBOUR PUBLISHING

Published by
Harbour Publishing Co. Ltd.
P.O. Box 219, Madeira Park, BC V0N 2H0
www.harbourpublishing.com

Cover and text design by Martin Nichols
Cover photograph of Redwood National Park by Getty Images,
photographer Alanie/Life File
Printed and bound in Canada

THE CANADA COUNCIL | LE CONSEIL DES ARTS
FOR THE ARTS | DU CANADA
SINCE 1957 | DEPUIS 1957

BRITISH
COLUMBIA
ARTS COUNCIL
Supported by the Province of British Columbia

Harbour Publishing acknowledges financial support from the Government of Canada
through the Book Publishing Industry Development Program and the Canada
Council for the Arts, and from the Province of British Columbia through the British
Columbia Arts Council and the Book Publisher's Tax Credit through the Ministry of
Provincial Revenue.

Library and Archives Canada Cataloguing in Publication

Carder, Al, 1910–
    Giant trees of Western America and the world / Al Carder.

    Includes bibliographical references and index.
    ISBN 1-55017-363-4 / 978-1-55017-363-5

    1. Trees. I. Title.
SD373.C37 2005   582.16   C2005-903970-1

Contents

Preface

My interest in trees started during the First World War—in 1917 to be exact. Father was a railroad man working for the Great Northern Railway, which ran through Cloverdale, a village in the lower Fraser Valley, 40 miles east of Vancouver. The attack on the virgin stands of timber in the area was already underway, but there were many untouched tracts remaining. Dotted over the cutover lands were the occasional enormous standing trees, possibly left because they were too big and expensive to handle. My father would take me in the railroad handcar and while pumping would wave and point out when we passed a tremendous lone Douglas-fir whose top on overcast days would seem to touch the low-hanging clouds. I have never forgotten those trips.

Later, when automobiles came into use, I remember one spectacular tree, a Douglas-fir, on the east bank of the Fraser River. This stood a mile or so upstream from where the railroad-cum-highway bridge spanned the river. If one stood on the bridge and looked northeast, the tree dominated the view. In fact, it could be observed from the city of New Westminster if one climbed the hill behind the town. This, of course, was several miles distant, but even from there the tree stood out as a genuine landmark. It had its own five-acre plot set aside for it known as Timberland Park. It was said to be 300 feet high, flat top and all, and it towered majestically above the diminutive second growth nearby.[1] It was just off the Pacific Highway connecting Vancouver with the United States, and motorists could turn off the road for a close up view of the solitary giant. Since it was ancient, judged to be 600 years old, it was known to drop a limb occasionally. This posed a hazard and in time the tree was taken down.

By the late 1920s there was only one large tract of virgin timber left in the entire lower Fraser Valley. This consisted of about one square mile in the municipality of Surrey and it was called the Green Timbers. The Pacific Highway ran through it, first as a gravel road and then paved after 1923. This forest of giant trees was expansive enough to create a climate of its own. Under certain conditions thin veils of cloud drifted high up among the trees while the farming country around was clear and cloudless. After the road was paved I would bicycle several miles to the stand of trees and walk into it, as to me it was a mysterious realm, a place of wonder.

The Green Timbers was not an ancient forest. I do not remember much debris on the ground except for the odd badly rotted mossy log, and the boles of the trees were only six to seven feet thick. It was the height of the trees that enthralled me. Their loftiness was enhanced by the vine maples that grew among their shaftlike boles, which rose for 100 feet or more above them before branching out to form the topmost canopy. Through this the rays of the sun would filter down to shimmer on the vine maple leaves only 30 feet above my head. Below all was the forest floor made green by the ferns and other beautiful leafy plants. Here I would stand in awe and gaze at the grandeur of the scene and think of the amazing Power that brought all this about. It stirred the innermost sanctum of my soul.

The Green Timbers were cut down in 1930, a singularly stupid act based on greed. The timber people brought out all sorts of arguments why the trees should come down, and down they came, despite being such a superb tourist attraction! But this was not the real reason one should deplore the idea of cutting them down. Such a stand of trees has a profound effect on the mind, the body and the soul of all who view them. Nonetheless, the timber barons had their way, and no members of the local government had either the astuteness or the fortitude to raise a voice to stop the plunder.

There were dissenters, however. One, Sam Hill, an industrialist of another country, the United States, spoke up to save the trees, but nobody of authority listened to him. Sam Hill was a successful businessman associated with the Great Northern Railway, which at the time was one of the leading transportation systems in the world. His words of wisdom were ignored by the local insipid minds that professed to run things.

It is profoundly sad that Canada was not blessed with visionary men such as Theodore and Franklin Delano Roosevelt of the United States. Instead, the magnificent southwest coastal forests of British Columbia were given over to men of narrow outlook and self-interest.

In 1932 I was a student attending the University of British Columbia, Vancouver. While staying in the city I took the opportunity to visit old family friends, Mrs. Watkins and Harry Bennett. Harry was a bachelor who worked as a barber downtown and roomed and boarded at Mrs. Watkins' home. After the evening meal, Mrs. Watkins asked if I would like to go with her and Harry to visit the Hilands, who lived in Shaughnessy Heights, a choice upscale district of Vancouver. Mrs. Watkins, a widow, was in some way related to the Hilands, whose interest was logging in rather a big way. Hiland could be termed a timber baron. Mrs. Watkins knew that I was very interested in plants, as my studies at the university were directed along that line. Plants included trees, and she said a Mr. MacMillan, a forester, would be there and perhaps he would be able to answer questions about trees. So I accompanied Mrs. Watkins and Harry to the Hiland home for a social.

Did I learn anything about trees? It was an exercise in futility. Soon the social party split into two groups and retired to different alcoves of the big drawing room. I gravitated to the men, Messrs. Hiland, MacMillan and Bennett. The older men opened up conversation and soon the talk drifted to forestry. When Douglas-fir was mentioned I put forward a question or two. My questions were brushed aside as of no consequence. Hiland and MacMillan (Harvey Reginald) started talking business, which largely involved how and where to obtain choice tracts of timber for logging. Harry edged off and joined the ladies and I soon did likewise as I could see that this was not the place I was going to gain any meaningful information on the subject of trees. All that Hiland and MacMillan appeared to be interested in were schemes to advance their fortunes. MacMillan seemed to lead in this. Hiland, I knew, was already well off.

This occasion left me with a poor feeling in my heart for Mr. MacMillan. I have little against a person having wealth, but I do not condone making it by raw exploitation. I went my way, doing research with plants, while he went his.

Some years after the MacMillan incident I graduated from college and entered my life's work. This had to do with plants, of course, but was carried out in areas of the world sparsely inhabited by trees, at least truly noticeable ones. Forty years went by—years of work, war and family—and the subject of trees was pushed aside through all this time, but the interest remained. It wasn't until I returned to my homeland that the much cherished subject arose again. One fine August day I sat on a rock in the forest near the shore of Vancouver Island's west coast. Through the trees came the gentle swish and sigh of the waves upon the sand. The late afternoon sun shone warmly and I began to dream. Where were the giant trees my father showed me 60 years ago? Were there any left? I launched a search.

There was the Koksilah Tree, a gigantic Douglas-fir that grew in the valley of the river of that name on southeast Vancouver Island. The tree had been there for over 700 years, as shown by its growth rings. When the loggers came in the late 1960s it was 320 feet high, not by any means the tallest tree ever measured in British Columbia, but possibly the tallest at that time. It had a trunk diameter of 12.7 feet at a man's breast height and its straight columnar bole was clear of branches for 110 feet up.

Retired old-time logger Gordon Baird led me to the tree in 1977 when it stood virtually alone. The magnificent forest had been extensively clear-cut for miles around, and this lone tree was a spectacular sight. Its top had already been blown off during the clear-cutting, and after our visit the whole tree blew down. At the time we visited it there were no directional signs to the tree, but after it was down a sign appeared and a parking lot for cars was provided. Posts were driven in along the full length of the prone trunk so that visitors could be guided as they walked along it to view and admire what "once was."

Looking back on all this, I find it difficult to believe that human beings were so driven by greed as to close their eyes to this exceptional gift that nature had provided. The wealth that the timber produced is paltry compared to what the country as a whole would have been blessed with had the tree been preserved—and it is not only a case of money. A square mile of the surrounding trees should have been left as buffer, for from the size of the stumps it must have been an exceptional forest.

When Gordon Baird showed me the Koksilah Tree I measured its height by clinometer. It stood on a five-foot pedestal of its own making, a buildup of bark fragments, cones, cone scales and needles that had accumulated over the centuries. I took the height measurements from the ground. I wrote the logging company about the tree. They said that they were very proud of it, but apparently not enough to do anything to preserve it. They said that their measurements showed it to be 315 to 325 feet high and 750 years old. Gordon and I found the blown-off top and measured it. After the tree blew down in the winter of 1979, Jerry Gardiner, a tree enthusiast, and I checked the face of the break at the tree's top with that of the blown-off portion to make sure it really was the tree's top that had been measured before. We also measured the length of the prone tree by tape. This measurement confirmed that of the clinometer.

In some ways greed is good, as our very evolution is based on it. But we are thinking beings and should exercise control; if this had been done, much, much more would have been gained than the miserable amount immediately obtained.

For a number of years recently I drove back and forth several times each week along the road between Victoria, on the southern tip of Vancouver Island, and Sooke, a town 20 miles to the west. It is a winding, rather pretty road set in hills and bordered by rock outcrops and trees of various kinds including alders, bigleaf maples, giant poplars, firs and red cedars. One straight, flattish stretch could have been boring but was relieved by two lofty Douglas-fir trees, side by side, slim and straight, nicely verdured with long cylindrical boles arising from the roadside scrub. Behind them lay a nondescript tract of timber extending up a slope. It had been logged in a hit-and-miss fashion years before and now the second-growth waited to catch the eye of some entrepreneur. As expected, logging soon began. For a while the two outstanding trees were left and I wondered whether they might actually be on the road's right-of-way. I fervently hoped so. It was an uplifting sight to enter that humdrum stretch of road and view them, especially in the winter when ground fog encircled their shaftlike boles and their heads loomed higher than ever. But I remained apprehensive that they would be erased from my sight. My pessimism was induced by long experience that had given me a very clear insight into what controlled the logging industry, both the "gyppo" and the corporate kind. For them the beauty of the natural world counts for virtually nil, as does the public good. The sole motivation is profit. On my next trip the trees were gone. Ah, Greed, how kind you are!

This book is the descendant of one I published in 1995 entitled *Forest Giants of the World, Past and Present*. After its publication I was asked a number of times exactly how the giant trees of British Columbia compare with those elsewhere in the world. It was always understood that the questioner was referring to the giant trees of the past, before the advent of the logger. It was difficult to answer these questions because few people paid close attention to the giants in those days—they were so common that they were rarely measured, resulting in a serious dearth of records. However, with the skimpy data available it is obvious that the present forest and its giant trees in no way represent what once was. The records presented here are measurements that have survived and that have some credibility or can be verified. There may well have been even bigger trees that were simply never measured.

Ideally, such a book should have been written a hundred years ago, but no one assumed such a venture until the 1980s when Randy Stoltmann, a determined and adventuresome young man, took on the task. His work was astoundingly good but was curtailed in May 1994 by a fatal accident on one of his exploration trips. Robert Van Pelt, Big Tree Coordinator for Washington State, came to the fore in the 1990s. He has been doing excellent work in British Columbia, although his main focus of study is in the states to the south. Currently active in British Columbia are Ralf Kelman, Shaun Muc, Adrian Dorst and others.

The tree records from other parts of the world, used as a comparison to those of British Columbia, also include records of trees of the past.

Acknowledgements

This tree book would have got nowhere without the support of my wife, Mary, who acts as my communicator because I am largely deaf due to age. I am also deeply thankful to my daughter, Mary-Clare, who computerized my longhand efforts. This compilation of facts would not have been possible without the reports made available to me by all the big-tree measuring people throughout the world.

For British Columbia, I relied on the many records of the late Randy Stoltmann and those of the currently active big-tree hunters and measurers. I have received great assistance from the tree loving people working in the Pacific Coast states to the south. Robert Van Pelt of Washington, through his recent book, *Forest Giants of the Pacific Coast*, has been of paramount assistance. He also helped me as I worked along on the write-up. I am grateful also to such workers as Brian O'Brian and Frank Callahan of Oregon and Ron Hildebrant of California.

I wish to express my deep appreciation to Audrey McClellan, whose editorial expertise greatly improved the content of this book.

Of course I referred to my previous book, *Forest Giants of the World*, and I would like to thank all those who helped in its creation, such as the late Alan Mitchell (England), Luigi Scaccaborozzi (Europe), Ken Simpfendorfer and Jack Bradshaw (Australia), Stephen Harris (Tasmania), John Halkett and John Salmon (New Zealand), Timothy Whitmore (Tropics) and Eve Jenkins (*née* Palmer) and C.J. Esterhuyse (South Africa), plus many others.

Introduction

Industrial man has produced great changes in the forests of British Columbia and many other parts of the world. The Douglas-fir, British Columbia's leading tree, has been devastated, as have the giant eucalypts of Australia and many tree species of Central and South America, tropical Africa and southeast Asia. In this book, I attempt to describe what existed before man's destructive interference and to compare the historic giant trees of British Columbia with those of the rest of the world.

To emphasize differences, the outstanding all-time known champion of each species of these giant trees is brought forth from the forest in a drawing made to scale so it can be compared with others. The drawings depict the awesome giants, the remarkable trees. Also shown are the champions of tree species that are less remarkable but still very noticeable in a forest setting. The little folk at the trees' bases are 1.8 metres (6 feet) high and function as a measuring stick.

Of the 45 drawings, all are on the same scale except Figure 19, the common or English yew, *Taxus baccata*, which has been given a magnification of twice that of the others. It should be noted also that the drawings represent the maximum dimensions (height, diameter, etc.) ever attained by the species, even though in nature such sizes are usually found in different individual trees.

What constitutes a "remarkable tree"? Foremost would be an attribute that in everyday parlance may be termed a "walk stopper" or a "jaw dropper"—one that produces a reaction in the observer. It may be just the size of the tree, particularly the width of its trunk or its height, but other features also come into play, such as the length of clear bole to where the branches begin or the size and span of the branches. Signs of great age may also arouse attention. In this study, certain requisites are necessary, such as the following:

1. The tree has a bole 3.7 metres (12 feet) or more in diameter at or near a man's breast height.
2. The tree is 61 metres (200 feet) or more tall.
3. It has a crown span of at least 46 metres (150 feet).
4. It is at least 1,000 years old.
5. It has some unusual quality, such as massive buttressing.

All these features are related to the "eye appeal" of the tree. Volume of wood contained is not listed, even though it is an important criterion of size. Currently there is insufficient data to warrant its use in a worldwide study.

If a species has produced a tree that exhibits even one of the above features, it may well fall into the "remarkable tree" category. Then there are species of trees that produce individuals that are not really remarkable, and yet are distinctly noticeable. A selection of these is presented here in the chapter "Trees of Lesser Stature."

Remarkable Trees of British Columbia and the Pacific Northwest

Douglas-fir

Pseudotsuga menziesii

Figure 1 shows a sketch of a giant Douglas-fir. This could well be the Lynn Valley Tree, the tallest authentically measured Douglas-fir.[2] Unfortunately there are no photographs of that tree available. The only one I ever saw was taken after it was felled, and that photo has disappeared. So although the sketch is drawn to scale—126.5 metres (415 feet) high, with a bole 4.3 metres (14.2 feet) in diameter at breast height—its branch arrangement borrows that of another very tall Douglas-fir of which there is a photo. This latter tree was blown down shortly after the photo was taken.

In 1896 a giant fir was brought down by loggers in the Kerrisdale district, South Vancouver. Its measurements were just a little less than the Lynn Valley Tree, though its exact height seems never to have been recorded. Julius M. Fromme, the superintendent of Hastings Mill where it was handled, declared it to be the biggest tree he had ever seen and it was "about," "nearly" or "just short of" 122 metres (400 feet) long and 4.2 metres (13.7 feet) in diameter of bole, exclusive of the bark.[3]

The Lynn Valley Tree was known as the biggest tree ever felled in Lynn Valley, but this was a locality of super trees and there were other huge and tall trees there, some with trunks 4 metres (13 feet) or more thick. One on the slender side was so fine a tree that the timber people who handled it took the time to measure its total length, which had little to do with their overriding interest: the amount of lumber they could get out of it. From this tree, only 3 metres (9.7 feet) thick at the butt, 16 pieces, each 4.9 metres (16 feet) long, were cut. The top 28 metres (92 feet) were discarded. The tree had no branches for 67 metres (220 feet) up and its total height was 107.3 metres (352 feet).[4]

So much for trees measured and recorded; but British Columbia also had a mythical tree—the Cary Fir. This was a huge Douglas-fir supposedly felled by George Cary, a local logger, in Lynn Valley in 1895. The story began as a hoax in 1922, supported by faked statistics: overall length of 127.2 metres (417 feet), diameter of stump 7.6 metres (25 feet), height to first limb 91.5 metres (300 feet), diameter of bole at first limb 2.75 metres (9 feet), thickness of bark 41.9 centimetres (16.5 inches), age 1,800 years. The claim was refuted by George Cary and others, but British Columbians' desire to believe they once possessed the world's tallest tree was such that the myth persisted and was difficult to arrest. In fact, the alleged dimensions of the tree were not so exaggerated as to be beyond belief, as exemplified by the Lynn Valley Tree and others.[5]

The foolery of prestige can on occasion obscure the truth. We have on one hand Major J.S. Matthews, who for a period was the unofficial archivist for Vancouver and later the official archivist. On the other hand there was Walter MacKay Draycott, an amateur naturalist who lived in Lynn Valley. Both, because of their respective activities, became acquainted with the giant and awesomely tall trees that stood where Greater

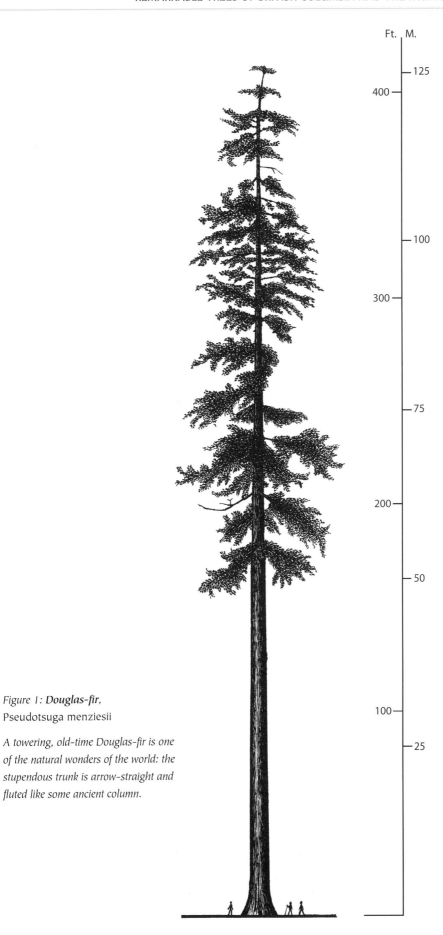

*Figure 1: **Douglas-fir**,*
Pseudotsuga menziesii

*A towering, old-time Douglas-fir is one
of the natural wonders of the world: the
stupendous trunk is arrow-straight and
fluted like some ancient column.*

Ft. M.

125
400
100
300
75
200
50
100
25

Vancouver is now. Matthews was a man-about-town type, very interested in all that went on. He liked to gather information, much of it by verbal contact. Draycott assembled information too. He delved into all that was around him, not only humankind, but also matters relevant to nature, such as wildlife, trees, plants, insects, soils, rocks, weather and artifacts. He published two books about his locality, both well received by those interested in such matters. He was aided in this by two attributes: some spare time to spend on his life's interests and a very long life of good health and a sound mind. He died at the age of 102 years. However, it was Matthews and what he had to say and record that drew attention. I am not sure whether this was because he bore the title "Major" or because he was a very loquacious man.

Both Matthews and Draycott had heard of the Cary Fir story and all its details. Both recognized it for what it was—a hoax. But only Draycott was able to separate it from the giant Douglas-firs, such as the Lynn Valley and Kerrisdale trees, that actually existed. Draycott did his best to cleave fact from fiction, but few listened.[6] Matthews dreamed up a story that the BC loggers' Hoo-Hoo Club had fabricated the Cary Fir measurements to fool members of the Washington chapter of the club. This satisfactorily debunked the Cary Fir, and in the process he refuted all reports of similarly sized Douglas-fir trees. It is now known that there were some around, but people were only interested in the dimensions of Cary's Paul Bunyan tree.

An ancient giant Douglas-fir at one time stood near the small town of Cloverdale, now a suburb of Vancouver. William Shannon came upon it in 1881 when he was cutting out what was then known as the Hall's Prairie Road. The tree was inordinately big and tall, and after it was felled Shannon measured it. Shannon came to the country in 1862 and in 1906 was interviewed in Vancouver by a newspaper reporter, as by that time he was known as a logging pioneer and timber expert. When questioned he said, "Near Cloverdale I measured one giant fir that after felling was 358 feet long and eleven and a half feet across the stump. I counted the circles and calculated that the tree had been growing for eleven hundred years."[7] My father knew the Shannon family well and had the tree described to him.

In 1920 my father and I visited the old Vancouver Museum at Hastings and Main streets. There, next to the curator's desk, was a small side table and on it was a photograph showing about 15 metres (50 feet) of the butt end of an enormous felled tree. It was not the picture that held our attention, however, but the caption beneath. This said that the length of the fallen giant was 125 metres (410 feet). We did not know it at the time, but this was a picture of the Lynn Valley Tree. My father and I discussed this great length on the spot because the tallest tree we had heard of was the Shannon Tree near Cloverdale, where we lived. My father then said that 122-metre (400-foot) trees could be possible in Lynn Valley on the North Shore, as there was less wind there.

Going south into Washington State, there were also several exceptionally tall Douglas-firs recorded. The best known is the Mineral Tree, which at one time stood near the town of Mineral in the foothills of the Cascade Mountains. This tree was measured in two sections, as its top had been blown off before it was viewed by a man capable of measuring it. Joe Westover, a "land engineer" from the Northern Pacific Railway, found and measured the downed top in 1905. It was 51.2 metres (168 feet) long. He then estimated the standing part to be 70.1 metres (230 feet), making a total height of 121.3 metres (398 feet) or, as he said, the tree was nearly 400 feet (122 metres) high originally. However, in 1924 Richard McArdle, a trained forester, measured the standing part by instrument and found it to be 68.6 metres (225 feet) high. Thus the true total height is 119.8 metres (393 feet).[8] Another fir not far away, known as the Nisqually Tree, in the drainage basin of the river of that name, was measured by a party of surveyors in 1900 while taking inventory of Douglas-fir forest in the area. This was a downed tree and its long branch-free stem drew their attention. Their tape showed that the length of the tree was 115.9 metres (380 feet) despite a small piece of top missing.[9] Farther north, close to the Canadian border, a Douglas-fir was felled near Sedro-Woolley that was 106.7 metres (350 feet) high.[10] There is also the report of a giant Douglas-fir felled in 1903 in the Willapa Hills near the town of Pe Ell and known as the Pe Ell Tree. It was 103.7 metres (340 feet) tall with a stump 4.9 metres (16 feet) thick at breast height.[11] The tallest fir standing today is in Oregon, the Brummitt Fir, at 100.3 metres (329 feet).[12] The top 3.7–4.6 metres (12–15 feet) of this tree is now dead. The tallest piece of live foliage on a Douglas-fir is a beautiful specimen in Prairie Creek Redwoods State Park in California. The 99.1-metre (325-foot) tall tree has a large healthy crown and is still growing.

Some of the notable Douglas-firs had substantial girths. An ancient giant on the east coast of Vancouver Island, known as the Westholme Tree, was toppled by a storm in 1919. It had a trunk 5.2 metres (17 feet) thick at 1.2 metres (4 feet) above the ground.[13] The Kerrisdale Tree, assuming that Julius Fromme, being a true mill man, measured the thickness of the wood only, would be at least 4.9 metres (16 feet) in diameter at the butt. Fromme's measurement was 4.2 metres (13.7 feet), and the bark was said to be 41 centimetres (16 inches) thick. The bole of the Mineral Tree in Washington was considered to be 4.9 metres (16 feet) at a man's breast height before strips of bark were torn off by fishermen to make a fire to keep warm.[14] The Clatsop fir in Oregon had a trunk diameter of 4.7 metres (15.5 feet). Perhaps the granddaddy of all in the Douglas-fir line was the Conway Snag in the Puget Sound area. Its trunk was 5.5 metres (18 feet) thick at 1.5 metres (5 feet) above the ground.[15]

These gargantuan Douglas-firs were ancient. The annual rings of a time-worn giant in Lynn Valley were counted at 1,280 years.[16] The Westholme Tree was about 1,500 years old when downed by storm. It was not possible to make an accurate count due to butt rot.[17] A sound tree in Washington, known as the Finney Creek Tree, had 1,400 rings when felled by man.[18]

To gaze at a towering, old-time Douglas-fir is to see one of the wonders of the world. The stupendous trunk, shaftlike and clear of branches for 45 metres (150 feet), arrow-straight and fluted for its entire length like some ancient column, astonishes the observer. The bark is a dark, greyish brown, contrasting nicely with the deep green needlelike foliage held far up against the sky.

If someone wants to see old-time giant coastal Douglas-firs it is best to visit an absolutely unlogged area. These are virtually extinct, but the best tract left is near

Quinault Lake, Washington State. Some of the mighty trees there have names such as the Rex, the Quamal, the Gatton Goliath and the Tichipawa. Some have an almost intact crown and are over 90 metres (300 feet) high, with a breast-height trunk diameter of 4 metres (13 feet) or more.[19] The only representative of a giant old-growth Douglas-fir in British Columbia is the Red Creek Tree atop a low ridge near the southwest coast of Vancouver Island. Sadly, a large part of its top was torn off by some ancient storm.[20]

A more imposing tree than the Red Creek specimen stood in the inland wilds of Vancouver Island up to 1979. This was called the Koksilah Tree, as it was in the drainage basin of the river of that name. It was 97.6 metres (320 feet) tall and had a breast-height trunk diameter of 3.9 metres (12.7 feet). It had been 750 years developing and over that time was protected by a stalwart forest of its peers. All the trees in the valley and slopes around were clear-cut in the 1960s and the Koksilah Tree was left virtually alone. Soon some 21 metres (70 feet) of its top were blown off, and a few years later the whole tree was cast down by storm—a fitting monument to the logging industry in British Columbia.[21]

Douglas-fir, the coast kind, is one of the great timber trees of the world, growing in extensive forests that stretch from south-central British Columbia through Washington and Oregon and into northern California.

Sometime during or prior to 1977, David Brock, an authority on the history of Vancouver, British Columbia, wrote:

> The world's tallest trees, accurately measured, are said to be the California coast redwoods, with the highest reaching just under 370 feet—although various eucalyptus trees have been reputed to grow to 375 feet, the biggest scientifically measured eucalyptus reached only 322 feet. A Douglas-fir felled in 1940 at Lynn Valley, in the Vancouver area, was properly measured at 417 feet. Loggers tell me that in Victorian times some bigger ones were almost certainly felled, not only in the suburbs but right in what is now downtown.[22]

Nowadays much more is known about these giant trees, not only in Vancouver and vicinity, but in other parts of the world. The tallest tree now standing is in the coast redwood groves of northern California and is dubbed the Stratosphere Giant with a height of 369.8 feet (112.7 metres).[23] The tallest redwood ever measured is the Eureka Tree of 380 feet (115.9 metres). It was logged out in 1914.[24] So in this instance David Brock, who made the above quote, was not far from the truth. His statement for the 375-foot (114.3-metre) height for the eucalyptus seemingly refers to the Cornthwaite or Thorpdale Tree. This was felled in 1880 and its measurement is now known to be genuine. However, there is an authentic measurement of a eucalypt 434 feet (132.3 metres) tall, the Ferguson Tree. This was measured after it had fallen across a deep ravine and so made the world's largest natural wooden bridge. William Ferguson, Inspector of State Forests, came upon it in 1872.[25] The 322-footer (98.2 metres) mentioned is a tree rather recently found in Tasmania. All these eucalypts are of the same species, *Eucalyptus regnans*, called in Australia mountain ash, in Tasmania swamp gum. With reference to the Douglas-fir in Brock's report, the 417-foot (127.1-metre) tree is the Cary Fir, a hoax, plain and simple. But a 415-foot (126.5-metre) tree was felled in North Vancouver in 1902. This is known as the Lynn Valley Tree and is the tallest authentically measured Douglas-fir.[26] As we have seen, it has some close runners-up in the Douglas-fir line.

Douglas-fir with its youthful drive and large gene base has presented the world with the occasional super tall tree, but only as a tree, not as a forest. Certain species such as the coast and Sierra redwoods produce grander forests.

Western red cedar

Thuja plicata

Western red cedar has an extensive range, starting at the extreme southeast section of Alaska, then south through coastal British Columbia including all of Vancouver Island and on through Puget Sound, Olympic Peninsula and the Cascade Mountains of Oregon, almost to the border of California, with a scattering of stragglers along the coast of that state. Western red cedar also grows very lustily in the inland areas of mid- to southern British Columbia as far east as the western slopes of the Rocky Mountains and also in mountainous northwestern Washington, northern Idaho and northeastern Montana, but the giant trees referred to here are all within the coastal fringe.

People who like to view stumps, especially big ones, would do well to visit the coastal parts of British Columbia and Washington. Where the giant firs and spruce trees were cut, huge stumps remain, but the biggest of all are invariably western red cedar. Archivist Major Matthews tells of a party of eight young men and women dancing a quadrille in 1887 on the sawn-off top of a stump in what is now the west end of Vancouver.[27] Many a hollow stump was used by people for shelter. Some were made ready by adding a few boards to provide a home for a single person, but there were instances where families were accommodated. One stump house was fashioned with a kitchen, living room and bedrooms. All rooms need not be on one floor. The bedroom was at times upstairs or, more correctly, upladder. In the early days trees were cut high to avoid base flare. This permitted the fitting in of a second floor. Occasionally a stump would serve as a store or post office.[28]

Many years ago my wife, Mary, and I were in the Olympic National Park, Washington, trying to locate a big red cedar tree that we had heard about. After a fruitless search on a wrong trail we backtracked and finally, on pushing through thick underbrush, came up against a great wooden wall. Edging around this, we found an opening through which we squeezed and entered a cavelike place. Fortunately it was a brilliant day and there was some filtered light about. We moved through further narrow openings and came to additional roomy places. Indeed, in one we could look up as if we were at the bottom of a huge chimney. Our tree proved to be the one we were searching for—the giant red cedar just north of Quinault Lake. The breast-height diameter of this magnificent living tree, known as the Quinault Lake Cedar, was 5.9 metres (19.5 feet). Like many of these ancient trees it had a candelabra-type head (note sketch at left), but this did not take place until 24.4 metres (80 feet) up the huge bole, which had little taper.[29]

The cause of some red cedar trees producing multiple heads while others do not seems to be summer drought. Under severe drought conditions a tree's lead or leaders may die, and when plentiful moisture returns they are replaced by new growth. In a life that lasts for several centuries, such droughts can happen several times, resulting in a multiple headed tree, popularly referred to as a candelabra-type tree.

The Quinault Lake Cedar reached only 53 metres (174 feet) high to the topmost sprig of its multi-headed crown, but what height would it have attained had it grown as a single-spired tree? This, of course, does occur. One such in the Squaka Valley at the head of Jervis Inlet on the mainland coast of British Columbia proved to be 84.5 metres (277 feet) high. However, this tree was only 3 metres (9.7 feet) thick at breast height.[30]

The greatest breast-height diameter of the bole of a red cedar ever recorded was 6.8 metres (22.3 feet), that of the Ocosta Cedar felled near Grays Harbor, Washington, in 1906.[31] The Sointula Cedar, which was about the same size, was felled on Malcolm Island off the northeast coast of Vancouver Island in 1923.[32] The Kalaloch Cedar on the west coast of Washington is still living and is 6 metres (19.6 feet) across the trunk at breast height, but only 37.5 metres (123 feet) tall. It has a pronounced candelabra-type head consisting of a dozen major reiterations (upright secondary trunks) and countless lesser ones. According to Robert Van Pelt, a big-tree researcher, it is one of the gnarliest trees he has ever seen.[33]

Not many miles from the Hoh River on the Olympic Peninsula is the Nolan Creek Cedar. It stands as a lone time-worn sentinel. A number of years ago the heavily forested land around it was clear-cut, leaving it isolated and soon to be surrounded by an expanse of newly planted smallish trees. Both the Quinault Lake and Nolan Creek trees are near the end of their lifespan, with much dead wood and little live tissue, but south of Quinault Lake stands the Willaby Creek Tree, healthy, flourishing and outstandingly tall with a massive trunk. The same can be said of the Cheewhat Lake Cedar on the west coast of Vancouver Island. This tree is without doubt the most striking of all the huge red cedars known in the world today.[34]

Some of these immense red cedar trees that have endured through the centuries develop trunk bases below the breast-height line of almost unbelievable proportions. This apparently has no relation to whether they have multiple tops or not. A tree near

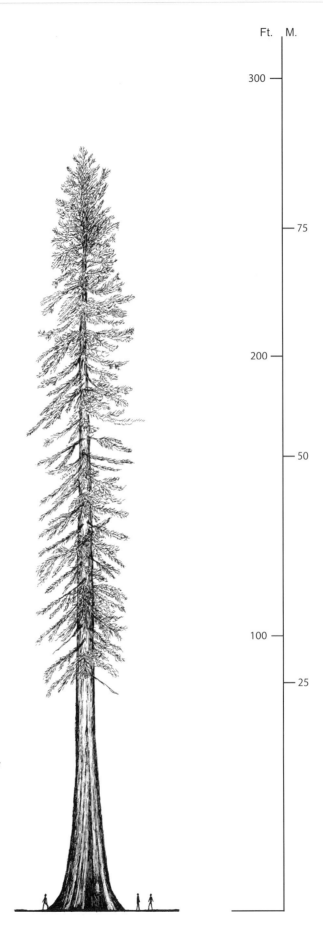

Ft.   M.

300 —

— 75

200 —

— 50

Figure 2: **Western red cedar**,
Thuja plicata

*Growing in competition with other tall
trees, such as Douglas-fir and Sitka
spruce, the lower branches of the
Western red cedar are sloughed off in the
shade, resulting in a clear trunk.*

100 —

— 25

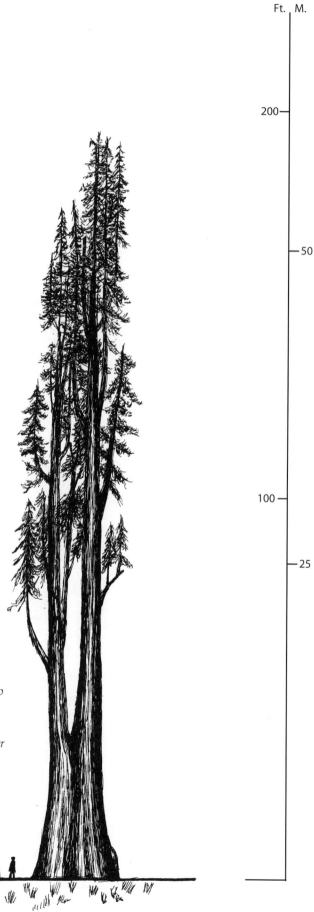

Ft. M.

200 —

— 50

— 100

— 25

*Figure 3: **Cheewhat Lake Cedar***

*The Cheewhat Lake Cedar is believed to
be 2,000 years old. The reason some
red cedar trees produce multiple heads
while others do not seems to be summer
drought. Over centuries, droughts
reoccur many times, resulting in a
candelabra-type tree.*

Seattle had a ground-line diameter of 16.8 metres (55 feet), rivalling the expansive bases of the giant sequoias of the Sierra Nevada. A vast hollow stump at Port Angeles, Washington, used for some years as a post office, had an outside basal diameter of 13.7 metres (45 feet). An outside diameter of about 9.8 metres (32 feet) is common for these cedars.[35]

Just what are the general features of western red cedar? The bark is cinnamon red in colour, thin, not more than 2.5 centimetres (1 inch) thick even on mature trees. It is stringy and can be pulled off in long strips. The leaves are tiny, scalelike, appressed and pleated, and are arranged in sprays. The cones, too, are small and are urn shaped, resembling small flower buds. They stand upright in clusters on the leaf sprays.

Figure 2 presents a single-spired western red cedar. It has the greatest height ever found for the species, plus the maximum diameter of bole for breast height and base—a rather exceptional tree, but shown to illustrate the maximum dimensions of the species. This tree, growing in competition with its peers and other tall trees, such as Douglas-fir and Sitka spruce, has sloughed off its lower branches because of shade and so has a clear trunk to 24.4 metres (80 feet), unusual for a red cedar, as they are not overly sensitive to shade. The lower branches droop, a feature of the species. Figure 3 represents the Cheewhat Lake Cedar, a candelabra type, which stands about 8 kilometres (5 miles) from the coast. Growth is very slow because of the cool summer temperatures near the ocean, so this tree is very old—there is good reason to believe that it has lived 2,000 years.

Sitka spruce

Picea sitchensis

There is no question that Sitka spruce is one of the largest trees of the world. Mature and aged trees usually have an enormous base structure. This is often the result of their beginning life on the stump or log of an ancient fallen monarch. The spruce roots straddle it and later coalesce, forming a massive base. The gigantic trunk may rise, branch free, through the thick, lower rainforest vegetation before becoming encircled with branches, but Sitka spruce does not generally have a tall shaft free of branches to a great height as Douglas-fir does. In a mature forest, the comparison is about 12 metres (40 feet) for Sitka spruce to 36 metres (120 feet) for Douglas-fir.

Two great Sitka spruce trees stand near the coast in Washington and Oregon. Both have damaged tops. The trunk of the Quinault Lake Spruce in Washington has a breast-height diameter of 5.4 metres (17.7 feet), while that of the Kloochy Creek Tree in Oregon is 5.1 metres (16.7 feet). Age estimates of these trees are about 600 years.

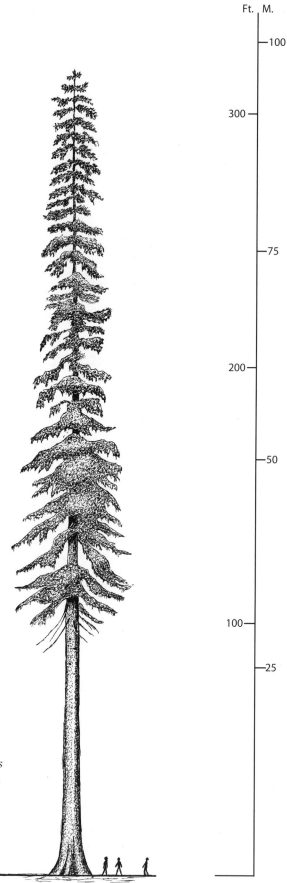

Ft.	M.
	—100
300—	
	—75
200—	
	—50
100—	
	—25

*Figure 4: **Sitka spruce**,*
Picea sitchensis

*This is an amalgam of the Carmanah
Giant and a singularly symmetrically
formed Sitka spruce in the Walbran
Valley. The Walbran Valley spruce is
known as Maxine's Tree, supposedly
named after a little girl who played at its
base while her father carried out studies
in the forest nearby.*

Although the Quinault Lake Spruce sets a record for size of bole, it is not the largest in volume of wood or overall size.[36] The laurels go to a fairly young tree, 350–400 years old, still growing vigorously and located at the Queets campground, Olympic National Park, and known as the Queets Spruce. It has a breast-height trunk diameter of 4.5 metres (14.9 feet) and a height of 75.6 metres (248 feet).

Many years ago, at the very beginning of the last century, a larger spruce than any now known was discovered. The height of this tree was estimated at 91.5 metres (300 feet), but the width of bole was carefully measured and this is what is arresting. Measurements made at 0.6 and 1.8 metres (2 and 6 feet) up from the ground indicate a breast-height diameter of 6.7 metres (22 feet). The tree stood in what is known as God's Valley, Clatsop County, near the coast of northwest Oregon. It was destroyed by fire soon after the measurements were made.[37]

Sitka spruce have huge base structures, but how tall can they reach? In the early years of the last century, while there were still some of the original tracts of forest left, surveys by the United States Forest Service in the Pacific states indicated that the tallest found was 90.2 metres (296 feet) high.[38] In British Columbia a number of years later an 87.2-metre (286-foot) tree was measured near Port McNeill on northern Vancouver Island.[39] In the early 1950s Bob Wood, a trail surveyor, observed a very tall spruce along the Hoh River trail in Olympic National Park, Washington, and his measurement showed it to be 92.1 metres (302 feet) high. This tree was known as the Schenk Tree and it blew down in 1953.[40] Later, in an especially beautiful grove of spruce in the Carmanah Valley, southwest Vancouver Island, a tree measured out at 93.9 metres (308 feet) tall.[41] In 1996 a tree in Queets Valley, Olympic National Park, was found with a height of 93 metres (305 feet).[42]

The most magnificent stand of Sitka spruce known today is in the Carmanah Valley mentioned above. Here a 95.7-metre (314-foot) tree, dubbed the Carmanah Giant, was found. It is more slender than many large spruces, having a breast-height trunk diameter of only 3 metres (10 feet), while trees 4 to 4.3 metres (13 to 14 feet) thick but less tall grow nearby. The Carmanah Giant was first measured by dropping a line from a hovering helicopter. This gave a height of 95.1 metres (312 feet). Later it was climbed and measured more exactly.[43]

Very slender and tall Sitka spruces are also found growing among the redwood forests of northern California. One called the Deep Valley Tree measured 96.6 metres (317 feet) tall but has since died back. It had a breast-height trunk diameter of only 2.1 metres (7 feet).[44]

Sitka spruce flourishes over a wide latitudinal range, from southeast Alaska to northern California. It thrives best near the sea, apparently benefitting from salt-laden winds.

Figure 4 is an amalgam of the Carmanah Giant and a singularly symmetrically formed Sitka spruce in the Walbran Valley, a defile next to the Carmanah. The rivers of both valleys flow into the Pacific Ocean. The Walbran Valley spruce is known as Maxine's Tree, supposedly named after a little girl who played at its base while her father carried out studies in the forest nearby.[45]

Yellow cedar

Chamaecyparis nootkatensis

Naturalists and foresters have long been interested in the great ages attained by trees. Any tree over 1,000 years old is regarded with a certain amount of deference, and although there is no conclusive evidence that a tree in British Columbia has reached 2,000 years of age, such a one would be an object of awe and study.

There are two species that could conceivably reach such an age: western red cedar (see p. 19) and yellow cedar. Large red cedars have been felled that showed annual ring counts up to 1,500 years, and there are much larger hollow giants whose age can only be guessed. The Cheewhat Lake Cedar, the largest red cedar in British Columbia, could be at least 2,000 years old, particularly since it is in an area noted for cool summers. Slabs of wood taken from nearby red cedars show annual rings exceedingly close together, indicating many years of age over a unit diameter of stem.

The wood of yellow cedar shows even closer growth circles, but this tree does not grow to the gargantuan size of red cedar. Still, its annual rings are so microscopically close that just 2.5 centimetres (1 inch) of radius can contain 360 rings. The bole of one tree with such close annual rings had a diameter of 1.7 metres (5.7 feet) and some of the larger trees in the area were up to 1.9 metres (6.4 feet) thick. These trees grew at quite high elevations, where the growing period is very short, and smaller trees—0.6 metres (2 feet) across—in the area were found to have lived 600 years.[46] Reasoning from these findings, it would seem that a tree with a bole 1.8 metres (6 feet) thick would exceed 2,000 years of age, allowing for slower growth as the tree ages.

Before logging, many yellow cedars grew in the Caren Range on the Sechelt Peninsula of mainland British Columbia. When this area was clear-cut there remained, of course, only trash and stumps. The oldest yellow cedar stump had 1,835 annual rings. This tree was perfectly healthy with no centre rot, and it seemed that it could have lived several centuries more. In an early investigation of yellow cedar, 3,500 years was thought to be a conservative estimate for maximum age.[47] This figure has been erroneously quoted as a ring count. Exhaustive research, however, may prove it not far from fact.

Yellow cedar likes its environment wet and cool. In the south of its range it is found at rather high elevations, from 610 metres (2,000 feet) up to the snow line, but farther north it is found lower, sometimes even at sea level. It is fairly common in southeast Alaska, on the Queen Charlotte Islands (Haida Gwaii), Vancouver Island and along the mainland coast, and in the Olympic Peninsula. It is also found high up along the western side of the Cascade Mountains as far south as southern Oregon. It seldom occurs in pure stands, but is often in small groves scattered among other tree species.

A number of giant yellow cedars have been found in British Columbia (Figure 5).

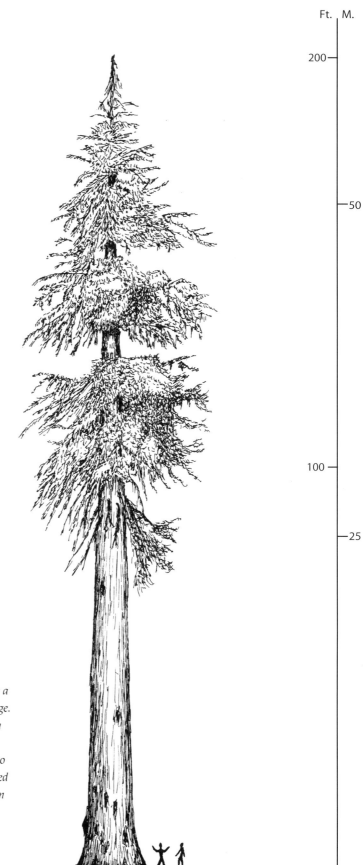

Ft. M.

200—

—50

100—

—25

*Figure 5: **Yellow cedar**,*
Chamaecyparis nootkatensis

In an early investigation of yellow cedar, 3,500 years was thought to be a conservative estimate for maximum age. In British Columbia, the oldest known yellow cedar stump had 1,835 rings. This tree was perfectly healthy with no centre rot, and it likely could have lived several centuries more, had it not been logged.

The champion stands near Kelsey Bay, Vancouver Island, and is 4.2 metres (13.7 feet) in bole diameter at breast-height and 61 metres (200 feet) high.[48] Another, in the Memekay River Valley not many kilometres away, has a 3.3-metre (10.9-foot) thick trunk and is 47 metres (154 feet) up to a damaged top.[49] These trees have only recently been discovered.

Near Quinault Lake, Olympic National Park, Washington State, there is a tree 3.7 metres (12 feet) in diameter and 37.8 metres (124 feet) high. This tree's bole is clear of branches for 24.4 metres (80 feet). It is thought to be over 2,000 years old.[50]

It is difficult to recognize a yellow cedar tree because its form is very like that of western red cedar. However, the branches are more droopy, with many small, loosely hanging branchlets. In this way yellow cedar trees are admirably adapted to shed snow. The crown is narrow and sharply conical, with the leading stem markedly pendent. The bole tends to be swollen at the base, sometimes with buttressing, and it can be somewhat fluted. The bark is a greyish brown, fibrous and ridged in long strips. It is thin, not more than 2.5 centimetres (1 inch) thick even on mature trees. The small appressed leaflets of the yellow cedar appear folded while those on the red cedar are more flattened. The fruiting bodies of these trees offer a better means of identification: the cones of the yellow cedar are spherical while those of the red cedar are ovoid, more bud shaped. Both are small, about 1 centimetre (0.4 inch) wide.

Black cottonwood

Populus trichocarpa

What is the tallest deciduous broadleaf tree species of the temperate regions of the world? It is black cottonwood, a form of poplar tree, also known as western balsam poplar. A tree of this kind, measured in the Puget Sound area of Washington, reached 68.6 metres (225 feet) high,[51] while another in the coastal forests of British Columbia was reported to be 70.1 metres (230 feet) tall.[52] No broadleaf deciduous tree outside the tropics is known to attain such towering heights. The closest contender is the tulip tree, *Liriodendron tulipifera*, of the forests of eastern North America, where two trees in the Smoky Mountains of North Carolina now stand at 54.6 metres (179 feet).[53] Taller trees up to 61 metres (200 feet) were measured in the past.[54]

Black cottonwood is a massive tree in every respect. The largest measured had a breast-height bole diameter of 3.8 metres (12.5 feet) while others had trunks that were branchless for 30.5 metres (100 feet) up.[55] The trunk is impressive—straight and cylindrical to a great height with bark 5 centimetres (2 inches) thick, narrowly furrowed

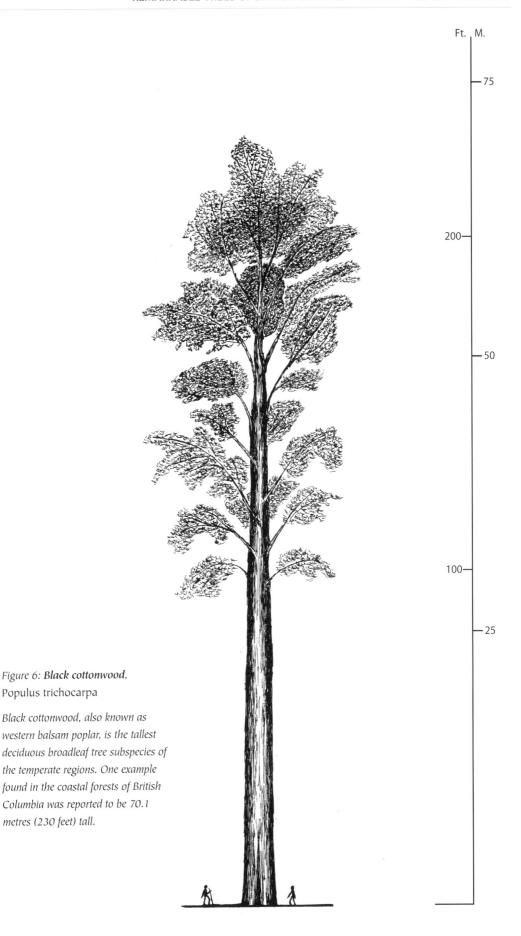

Figure 6: **Black cottonwood**,
Populus trichocarpa

Black cottonwood, also known as
western balsam poplar, is the tallest
deciduous broadleaf tree subspecies of
the temperate regions. One example
found in the coastal forests of British
Columbia was reported to be 70.1
metres (230 feet) tall.

and ridged. The tree has immense vigour and grows amazingly fast; it is not unusual for it to reach 30.5 metres (100 feet) tall in 20 years, but the exceptional individual that is 61 metres (200 feet) high or more must have special conditions to promote such height. It may sprout in a stand of coniferous seedlings where there is competition for light. For many years the cottonwood keeps abreast of, and even outdoes, its rivals, but in time the conifers overtake and pass on. Meanwhile, the cottonwood does its best in the quest for light and by such effort surpasses its usual height. Figure 6 shows a forest-grown tree in its prime. The trunk is branchless for a long way up and the lower branches are restricted more than they would be if the tree had been open grown.

The lifespan of black cottonwood is rather short, as you might expect for such a rapidly growing tree. Its maximum is about 250 years.[56] Long before this, however, the tree will show aging with broken limbs caused by storms, especially ice storms, to which it is highly vulnerable.

Black cottonwood is a tree of the Pacific Northwest coast from Alaska to California. Its best growth is in river valleys next to streams where there is an abundance of water and light. It may extend up river valleys for hundreds of miles from the coast. Without the special inducement, previously explained, to grow exceptionally tall, its height under favourable conditions is from 42.7 to 48.8 metres (140 to 160 feet) with a bole diameter of 1.2 to 1.8 metres (4 to 6 feet). The tallest today, as measured by laser, is 54.3 metres (178 feet) in the Queets River Valley. The large, heart-shaped leaves turn golden yellow in the autumn and present a beautiful sight. The name "cottonwood" comes from the fluffy down attached to the seeds to ensure their spread by wind.

Some botanists distinguish black cottonwood as a subspecies of balsam poplar, hence *P. balsamifera* ssp. *trichocarpa*. Black cottonwood hybridizes extensively with balsam poplar, but the latter does not have the giant-sized growth potential of black cottonwood.

Other Remarkable Trees of the World

NORTH AMERICA

Coast redwood

Sequoia sempervirens

Coast redwood is one of the remaining monsters of the past that still exists with little change. Unlike bygone monster animals, the tree has been able to find a refuge and lives well enough to this day. Granted, the refuge is small—a narrow locality almost totally in California, some 32 kilometres (20 miles) wide on average by 725 kilometres (450 miles) long, wedged between mountains on the east and the ocean on the west. The mid-latitude location and the lay of the land between a warm coast and a cold sea creates a summertime fog belt, a much-needed necessity for this tall tree to thrive. It not only flourishes but also produces some of the most stately and majestic forests on earth.

We should be thankful for having this wondrous creation from a past age. It must be handled with care as its race is deep set and not amenable to disruption and change. Although coast redwoods produce the tallest forests in the world, and probably have since the last ice age, they do not produce the tallest trees. This honour goes to species evolved nearer to our time, which are highly adaptive to change and have special spirally strengthening cells within their wood that give them added support to grow tall and outdo their competitors for sunlight and warmth.[57] This, unfortunately, has been their downfall, for it is this very feature that has made them attractive as structural timber to industrial man. Thus the finest stands have been logged out so that today the tallest standing trees are the coast redwoods, a wholly artificial scenario. (See Charts 1 and 2, pp. 136 and 137.)

Because coast redwood does not adapt well to change, its features tend to be uniform. For example, most tree species show variable maximum height, but not the redwood. The tallest tree for which reliable data are available—the Eureka Tree, logged out in 1914—was 115.9 metres (380 feet) tall.[58] Next is the Dyerville Giant at 113.4 metres (372 feet), felled by a storm in 1991. After it fell, observers noted that its root base was submerged in 1.5 metres (5 feet) of silt due to flooding, so the actual height of the tree was 114.9 metres (377 feet).[59] The tallest trees still growing are the Mendocino Tree in the Montgomery Redwood State Reserve, at 112 metres (367 feet),[60] and the recently discovered Stratosphere Giant in Humboldt Redwood State Park, 112.7 metres (369.8 feet) high.[61]

Chris Atkins and Michael Taylor have roamed the redwood forests and have found 126 trees between 106.7 and 112.8 metres (350 and 370 feet) high.[62] The reason for this

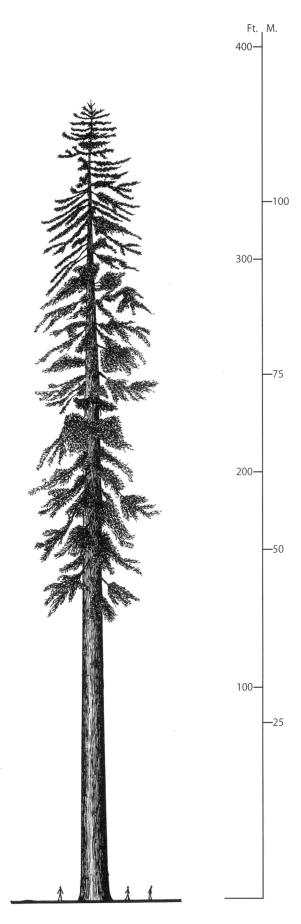

Figure 7: **Coast redwood**,
Sequoia sempervirens

*A grove of mature coast redwood trees
is a wonderful sight. This tree is 115.9
metres (380 feet) high with a trunk
diameter of 4.6 metres (15 feet). Stumps
of trees felled in the early days of logging
show greater dimensions, up to 9.1
metres (30 feet).*

extraordinary uniformity of maximum height is that coast redwood is a species subject to genetic senescence. The word "moribund" has been used to describe this race of trees, but this is too harsh a term. These trees are not about to pass away. However, one cannot be sanguine about their future as they seem unable to respond to changing conditions and they will thrive only as long as the current climatic regimen holds.

Figure 7 shows the form of a giant coast redwood. This tree is 115.9 metres (380 feet) high; it has a trunk diameter of 4.6 metres (15 feet), is free of branches for 45.7 metres (150 feet) from the ground, and it upholds a span of foliage of 21.3 metres (70 feet). Many of these dimensions are exceeded by exceptional trees. For example, the coast redwood with the thickest trunk is the Lost Monarch in the Jedediah Smith Redwoods State Park with a breast-height diameter of 7.7 metres (25.2 feet).[63] Because the species is noted for its uniformity, it is not surprising that at least a dozen giants of near this size exist. Stumps of trees felled in the early days of logging show greater dimensions, up to 9.1 metres (30 feet). The height of trunk up to the first branches can likewise be greater than 45.7 metres (150 feet). Charles Sargent talks of a tree whose trunk was free of branches for 70.1 metres (230 feet),[64] and the giant Eureka Tree was said to have a clear bole for 79.6 metres (261 feet).[65] The usual spread of crown is shown in the drawing, but this could be more, up to 30.5 metres (100 feet). What age these trees can attain is uncertain. The accepted maximum is 2,200 years but there is reason to believe, based on the latest findings, that this is too conservative a figure. Perhaps something over 3,000 years would be nearer to the truth.[66] Further research is needed.

A grove of mature coast redwood trees is a wonderful sight, with the great brown columnar trunks rising above the rich green carpet of ferns and undergrowth to the canopy high above, with here and there a break in the wall of foliage permitting a view of the topmost boughs more than 90 metres (300 feet) above. Through the branches and foliage of these tall trees the sun casts slanting beams, awing one with the immensity of it all. It is at a time like this that reverence overwhelms the beholder, and this is good.

Giant sequoia

Sequoiadendron giganteum

Here is another monster of the past that is still with us. The giant sequoia, also known as Sierra redwood, exists tenaciously on a even narrower footing than does its cousin, the coast redwood. No extensive forests of it now remain, and it exists in groves scattered along the western slopes of the Sierra Nevada from west of Lake Tahoe to east of the city of Porterville, 400 kilometres (250 miles) to the south. Some of these groves contain only a few trees, while others assume the dimensions of a small forest. Giant sequoia is the most massive tree on earth, although several other species, such as coast redwood, are taller, and a few species have a thicker trunk.

Giant sequoia and coast redwood, although cousins, appear outwardly quite different in both general form and type of foliage. The foliage of giant sequoia is scaly, narrow, awl shaped and not tightly appressed to the stem, while that of coast redwood is flat needles arranged comblike on opposite sides of the rachis, forming attractive sprays like those of fir or yew. Young giant sequoia trees have the shape of a very sharp spire. As they mature they assume the rounded classic form and lastly, after a millennium or two, they become spike topped or stag headed as the tree dies from the top down. This dieback may not be entirely due to age but to ground fire or lightning strike. Normally the topmost stem, the leader, loses its verdure and the tree becomes spike topped. Later the topmost branches die and the tree is said to be stag headed. Meanwhile the trunk and branches become thicker because of the added annual growth rings.

Figure 8 shows a giant sequoia tree at the maximum height ever measured for the species—105.8 metres (347 feet). This was the length of a fallen monarch.[67] The Mark Twain Tree, felled for timber in 1891, was said to be 100.9 metres (331 feet) high.[68] The maximum height of living trees is 93.6 metres (307 feet).[69] Trees with a thicker trunk than that shown in Figure 8 exist. Figure 9, the General Grant Tree, exhibits a trunk 8.8 metres (29 feet) in diameter at breast height.[70]

Since the giant sequoia carries its vast trunk well up, usually between 45.7 and 61 metres (150 and 200 feet) high, the gross volume, including wood and bark, contained in the trunk can be enormous—possibly the greatest in the world. On this basis the General Sherman Tree's trunk has a volume of 1,557 cubic metres (55,000 cubic feet).[71] This volume may have been exceeded by giant sequoias of the past. A snag known as the Burnt Monarch may have been larger, but there is not enough left of this tree to prove it.[72] There is evidence, however, that some of the biggest coast redwood trees felled for lumber long ago may have been even larger. One, known as the Maple Creek Tree, has been calculated as having a gross trunk volume greater than that of the General Sherman Tree, and it is contended that this was not the largest coast redwood felled in the early days of logging.[73]

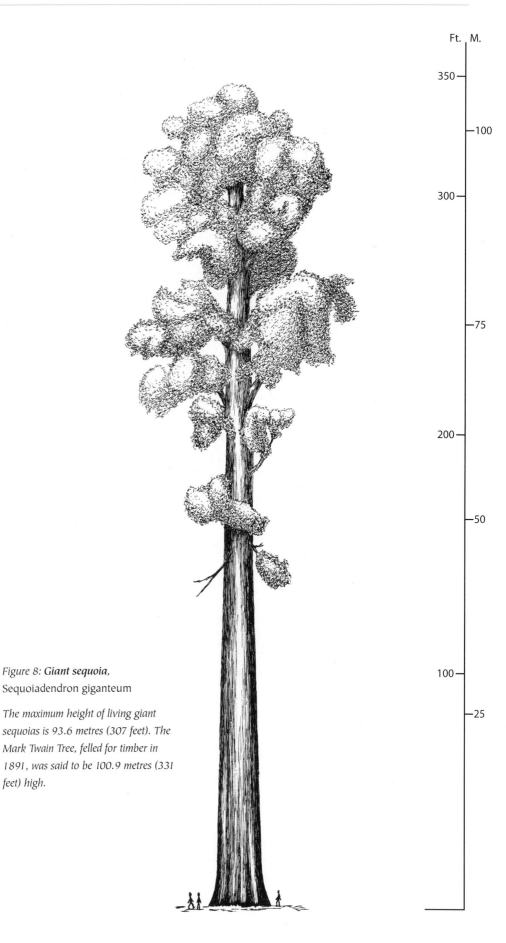

Ft.   M.

350 — 100

300 —

75

200 —

50

Figure 8: **Giant sequoia**,
Sequoiadendron giganteum

*The maximum height of living giant
sequoias is 93.6 metres (307 feet). The
Mark Twain Tree, felled for timber in
1891, was said to be 100.9 metres (331
feet) high.*

100 —

25

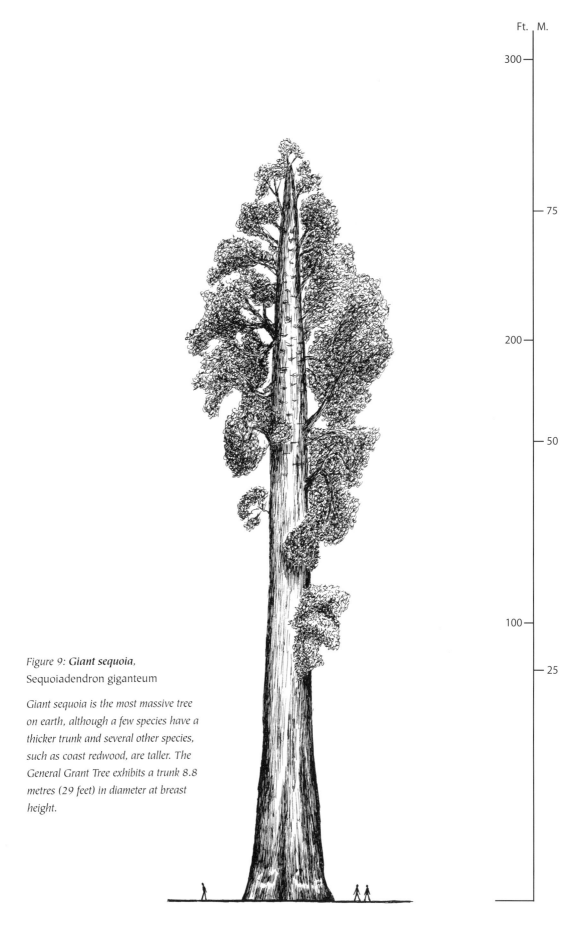

Ft. M.

300

75

200

50

100

25

Figure 9: **Giant sequoia**,
Sequoiadendron giganteum

*Giant sequoia is the most massive tree
on earth, although a few species have a
thicker trunk and several other species,
such as coast redwood, are taller. The
General Grant Tree exhibits a trunk 8.8
metres (29 feet) in diameter at breast
height.*

There is another way to compare the size of trees and that is to use the methods of the timber industry, which measure how much lumber can be got out of them. Because the bark of the giant sequoia is exceptionally thick, up to two feet or more on old trees, there is quite a difference between gross trunk volume and volume of merchantable wood. Some comparisons may be made using this latter factor. The trunk volume of the General Sherman Tree becomes 778.6 cubic metres (27,500 cubic feet). Some giant coast redwood trees, such as the Maple Creek Tree, had a merchantable lumber volume of 852.6 cubic metres (30,114 cubic feet), greater than that of the General Sherman tree because the bark of the coast redwood is thinner, being only about 20 centimetres (8 inches) thick on mature trees. (It seems that worldwide only the kauri pine of New Zealand (see p. 66) produces as much merchantable timber as the redwood.)

Coming upon a giant sequoia tree in the forest is a true walk-stopper: one stands and stares before moving on. It is the colossal rich reddish brown trunk that astonishes, as does the great height to where the branches begin. Figure 8 shows this to be 45.7 metres (150 feet), and this is not unusual. The age to which these trees live has been exaggerated, but close investigation indicates 3,500 years.[74] Giant sequoias do not live forever, and it is usually a storm that finally causes them to topple.

Noble fir

Abies procera

Noble fir is everything that its common name signifies. It can have a spectacular bole, perfectly cylindrical and branch free to a great height. This is because it is sun loving and the lower branches, when heavily shaded, slough off. One tree had a bole clear for 53.7 metres (176 feet).[75] A tree 99.1 metres (325 feet) high has been measured.[76] It was destroyed by the Mount St. Helen's eruption of 1980. The tallest known tree now is 89.9 metres (295 feet) high.[77] The maximum diameter of trunk at breast height is 2.9 metres (9.5 feet).[78] Above the stately clear bole, the branches reach out slightly downward and form an elongated, columnar crown (Figure 10). Noble fir is the largest of all the 51 true fir species. Its maximum lifespan is considerable—about 700 years.

The range of this valued tree is rather limited. It is classed as a subalpine species and the best stands are along the western slopes of the Cascade Mountains at elevations of 915 to 1,830 metres (3,000 to 6,000 feet) from mid-Washington south to mid-Oregon. Small stands of it also occur in the Coast Mountains of Oregon and in the Willapa Hills of southwestern Washington.

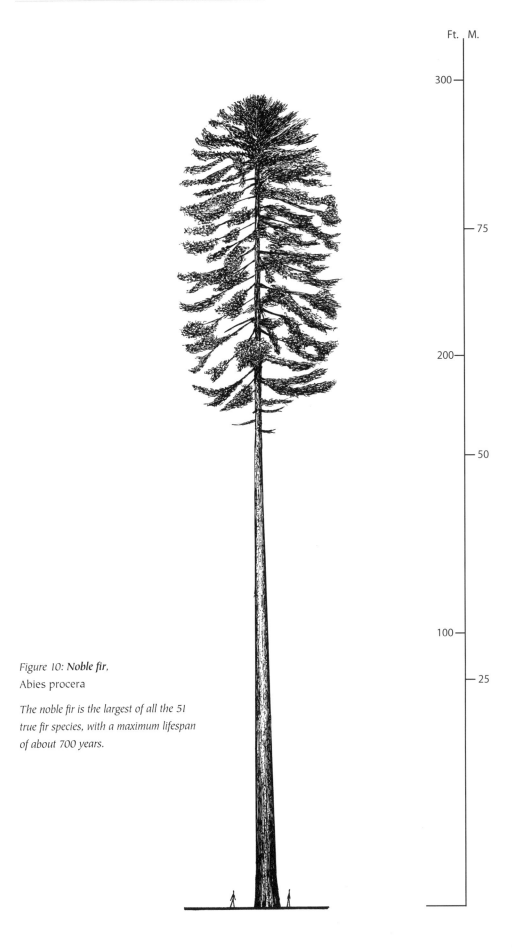

Ft. M.

300

75

200

50

Figure 10: **Noble fir**,
Abies procera

*The noble fir is the largest of all the 51
true fir species, with a maximum lifespan
of about 700 years.*

100

25

Sugar pine

Pinus lambertiana

The first sugar pine found and measured by a white man proved the biggest in width of bole of all specimens checked out since. It was searched out by the great Scottish plant explorer David Douglas in 1826 and it was a downed tree toppled by wind. Douglas's tape showed it to be 17.6 metres (57.75 feet) round or 5.6 metres (18.4 feet) in diameter 0.9 metres (3 feet) from the roots. Its full length was 65.5 metres (215 feet).[79] No tree of this species since found has a trunk this large so it is likely that there is an error of recording here. A tree with a breast-height trunk diameter of 4.6 metres (15 feet) was felled in the 1950s in the vicinity of Nickel Mountain, Douglas County, Oregon. This was an ancient tree considered to be a hazard. It was not milled because of "core rot." More recently a tree was cut down in Jackson County, Oregon, that had a bole 3.8 metres (12.5 feet) thick at breast height.[80] Robert Van Pelt in his hunt for giant trees describes five of the largest he found. One along the north fork of the Stanislaus River, California, has a breast-height diameter of trunk of 3.5 metres (11.5 feet), while another, in the Yosemite Valley of the same state, is 81.7 metres (268 feet) tall.[81] No living tree thicker or taller than these has ever been discovered.

Few kinds of tree, and certainly no other species of pine, have the majesty of the sugar pine. Its massive red-brown shaftlike trunk may rise branch free for over 30.5 metres (100 feet) above the lesser vegetation around, presenting a spectacular sight. Sugar pine normally lives from 300 to 500 years, but a 760-year-old tree has been found.[82] Its name comes from the fact that the pine's wounded trunk releases a sugary resin.

Figure 11 shows the actual maximum measurements of a sugar pine, except that the thickness of bole is quite a bit less than that of more ancient specimens. It was described by John Muir, the great naturalist, as the "King of Pines," an epithet that has never been disputed—quite an honour, considering that there are some 112 species of pine spread over many different parts of the world.

The feature that led David Douglas to his giant tree was the size of cones and the large edible seeds therein. Douglas had been shown these by the Indians while he was residing near the Columbia River, and he determined to find the tree that produced them. He tramped 160 kilometres (100 miles) south to view it and came upon it in central Oregon. The cones are huge—up to 60 centimetres (24 inches) long and about 10 centimetres (4 inches) wide—and they hang from branch ends, making them highly visible.

Douglas came upon his pine tree near the northern limits of its range. This was along the western slope of the Cascade Mountains. From there it extends south over the

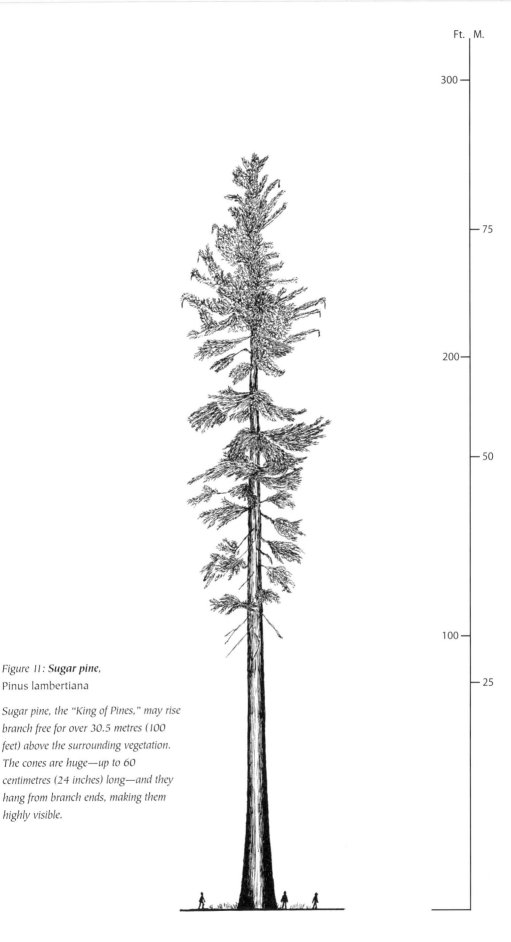

Ft. M.

300

75

200

50

Figure 11: **Sugar pine**,
Pinus lambertiana

Sugar pine, the "King of Pines," may rise branch free for over 30.5 metres (100 feet) above the surrounding vegetation. The cones are huge—up to 60 centimetres (24 inches) long—and they hang from branch ends, making them highly visible.

100

25

Siskiyou Mountains and follows the Sierra Nevada range to beyond central California. It rarely grows in extensive pure stands but is interspersed with other conifers, where it is a conspicuous tree even in the presence of giant sequoias.

The pine group has a long history, going back 100 million years. All species except one are indigenous to the northern hemisphere, and the exception—on the island of Sumatra—does not extend natively very far south of the equator.

Ponderosa pine

Pinus ponderosa

This is a tree of the dry country. It thrives in the rain shadows east of the mountain ranges that parallel the coast of western North America. It occurs in southern British Columbia east of the Coast and Cascade mountains, then south along the Cascades to northern California where it splits, with one division east of the Coast Mountains there and the other following the Sierra Nevada range to south-central California. In all this territory the biggest and tallest trees are found from mid-Oregon south.

Mature ponderosa trees have two noticeable features: distinctive yellow-brown bark arranged in sizeable plates, and long-needled foliage. They stand tall and are generally strikingly handsome (Figure 12). One, now logged, was 79.9 metres (262 feet) high, while another still standing has a bole thickness of 2.8 metres (9.1 feet).[83] The tallest tree living is said to be the Hartman's Bar Tree in California at 69.2 metres (227 feet), a most impressive specimen,[84] but Robert Van Pelt recently measured a tree of this species near Grant's Pass, Oregon, that scaled 78.6 metres (258 feet) high. The fact that the maximum measurements ever obtained in British Columbia are 50 metres (164 feet) for height and 1.8 metres (5.8 feet) for diameter of trunk[85] indicates that ponderosa likes conditions not only dry but also warm.

Ponderosa pine is long lived. The usual maximum age is about 700 years, but one tree showed a ring count of 1,047 years.[86]

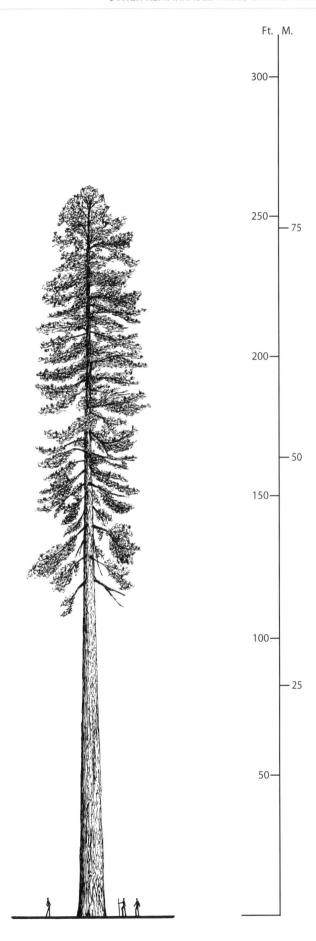

Ft. M.

300

250 ─ 75

200

─ 50

150

100

─ 25

50

Figure 12: **Ponderosa pine**,
Pinus ponderosa

*Mature ponderosa trees stand tall and
have two noticeable features: distinctive
yellow-brown bark arranged in sizeable
plates, and long-needled foliage. They
thrive in the rain shadows east of the
mountain ranges that parallel the coast
of western North America.*

Ft. M.

Eastern white pine

Pinus strobus

When the great naturalist John Muir gazed upon the sugar pine trees in the Yosemite Valley in 1868 he proclaimed the species to be the "King of Pines." He is right, but he might have been less dramatic had he viewed the vast forests of eastern white pine, *Pinus strobus*, before the settlers and loggers wrought havoc on them. The wood of this tree was so highly prized because of its many fine qualities—it could be easily worked, had straight grain and was warp free—that it was avidly sought and logged by the timber merchants. The finest stands had all but gone by the late 1800s. (See Chart 2, p. 137.)

Maximum size records for eastern white pine now standing indicate 2 metres (6.4 feet) for trunk diameter at breast height and 56.7 metres (185.9 feet) for height. This tree, in the Smoky Mountains of North Carolina, was originally 63.1 metres (207 feet) but its top was blown off. It is still the tallest known tree of the forest of the east.[87] About 100 years ago, in Muir's time, greater dimensions would have been expected but still not as great as in the primeval forest. There are quite a number of old-time records, some of which appear to be carefully obtained and documented. A few of the most authoritative are:

- A tree measured in 1705 in New Hampshire was reported to have a height of 79.9 metres (262 feet).[88]

- At Lincoln, New Hampshire, a tree had a trunk diameter of 1.8 metres (6 feet) and a height of 79.3 metres (260 feet), while another at Merrimack, in the same state and felled in 1736, measured 2.3 metres (7.7 feet) thick at the stump.[89]

- In 1899 a tree cut in Lycoming County, Pennsylvania, had a trunk diameter of 3.7 metres (12 feet) at the butt and was 61 metres (200 feet) tall.[90]

Confronted with such measurements, and comparing them to the height and diameter of existing trees, it is hard to believe they are true. When Henry Elwes, a prominent British arborist, came to North America in the early 1900s to view and study the continent's trees he thought to check out this very point. He had read about the Lincoln and Merrimack trees in *The Silva of North America* by Charles Sprague Sargent, the leading American dendrologist at the time. Elwes then wrote Prof. W.A. Buckhart of the Pennsylvania State College for clarification and Buckhart stated that the most authoritative record is by Fox, in the *United States Forestry Bulletin* no. 34, published in 1902, where he states "… there is a record of a white pine cut in Meridith, Delaware County, New York that measured 247 feet [75.3metres] in length as it lay on the ground."

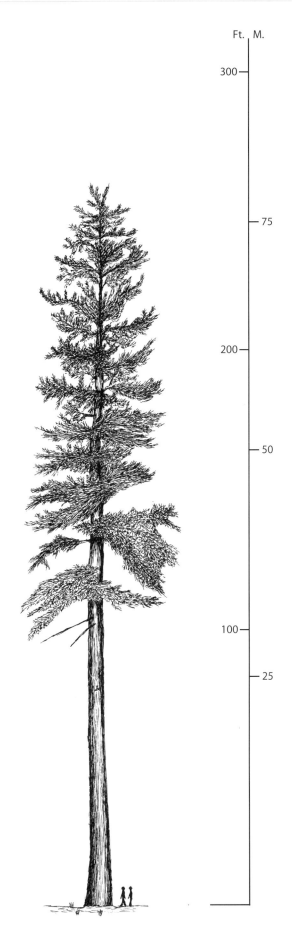

Ft. M.

300

75

200

50

100

25

Figure 13: Eastern white pine,
Pinus strobus

*Here is a drawing of a living eastern
white pine with some magnification
added to depict a giant of the past. The
western species is closely related but has
a narrower span of foliage with a more
pyramidal crown. The mature eastern
counterpart has a wider span of foliage
with a broadly rounded top and the
branches have a distinctive plumelike
out-throw from the bole.*

These measurements are not far short of those of the kingly sugar pine. Eastern white pine can be an arresting sight even today with its grey columnar trunk that may be free of branches for 30 metres (100 feet), surmounted by a dark verdant head of foliage held on branches that leave the trunk at right angles and have an upward sweep at the ends. Figure 13 is a drawing of a living tree with some magnification added to depict a giant of the past.

The records show that eastern pine can reach an age of about 500 years, as some felled trees have had a ring count near this number.[91]

This tree's domain is from Newfoundland to Manitoba, south through the northeast and Great Lakes states of the US and then along the Appalachian Mountains to northern Georgia.

Western white pine

Pinus monticola

Western white pine is closely related to eastern white pine (see p. 44) and can be regarded as the western equivalent of the eastern species. An interesting observation is that despite their close beginnings they have assumed quite different forms (note sketch, p. 47). The western species has a narrower span of foliage with a more pyramidal crown while the mature eastern counterpart has a wider span of foliage with a broadly rounded top and the branches have a distinctive plumelike out-throw from the bole. This variation in form has undoubtedly been induced over many millennia by the differences between their environments, including that of the immediate tree flora with which they have been associated. The western type has probably been exposed to heavier, wetter snowfalls as well as being more closely hemmed in by taller trees of its own kind and of other species. In nature these two kinds of trees have been separated by over 1,100 kilometres (700 miles) during and since the ice age.

Western white pine, as its specific scientific name implies, is a tree of the mountains, but in the northern parts of its range, such as British Columbia, it does come down to the seacoast, though seldom in pure stands. There it is mixed with Douglas-fir, western hemlock and other coastal trees. Its range under such conditions includes Vancouver Island, the immediate coastal mainland, the Olympic Peninsula and the Puget Sound area. From here it extends south along the Cascade and the Sierra Nevada mountains well into California. There are also vast forests of it far to the east in the western Kootenays of British Columbia and northern Idaho.

The biggest western white pine standing today is the Fish Lake Pine near Medford, Oregon. It is 67.7 metres (222 feet) tall with a breast-height bole diameter of 2 metres

(6.7 feet).[92] Taller and thicker trees have been measured in the almost pure pine stands of northern Idaho. Even now, after intensive logging, calamitous fires, devastating disease and insect attacks, trees can be found over 70 metres (230 feet) tall. A tree was once felled that yielded 73.2 metres (240 feet) of merchantable timber,[93] and trees have been measured with boles as thick as 2.6 metres (8.5 feet).[94] Near Lake Tahoe, California, stands a tree with a bole 3.2 metres (10.5 feet) thick, but it is a fusion of two smallish trees and is in no other respect spectacular.[95]

Even among the giant coastal trees, western white pine has features significant enough to make it conspicuous. The foliage is a dark bluish green. The needles are rather long, 5 to 10 centimetres (2 to 4 inches) in length, and are grouped in bundles of five. The cones are slender, 15 to 20 centimetres (6 to 8 inches) long, and hang down. Its bole, straight and cylindrical, can be free of branches for over 30.5 metres (100 feet). The thin bark, seldom more than 2.5 centimetres (1 inch) thick even on mature trees, is a very dark grey, almost black, ridged and edged in small rectangular plates.

Western white pine is long lived. It attains maturity in 200 to 350 years and occasionally lives for 500 years. A tree in British Columbia was found to be 615 years old.[96]

Western white pine (left) and Eastern white pine (right).

Port Orford cedar

Chamaecyparis lawsoniana

This is a majestic tree, also known as Lawson cypress. The largest specimen of which there is authentic record was 5.2 metres (17 feet) thick at the top of its 3.7-metre (12-foot) stump. After felling it was found to be 74.7 metres (245 feet) long, including the stump, and branch free for 54.9 metres (180 feet). It stood on a slope of the Upper Coquille River, Oregon (Figure 14).[97] There are no trees of this size now, the largest—the Elk Creek Champion—being 3.7 metres (12 feet) for thickness of trunk and 71.6 metres (235 feet) for height, although recently a taller tree of 72.9 metres (239 feet) was measured in the Coquille Falls area.[98] Since the wood of Port Orford cedar is fragrant, easily worked, strong and of great beauty, it has been heavily exploited. To make matters worse, its native range is quite limited, being confined to the southwest corner of Oregon and a small adjacent area in California.

The crown of Port Orford cedar is narrow with a nodding spirelike head. The branches are somewhat pendulous. The bark is reddish brown and fibrous. On mature trees it can be 25 centimetres (10 inches) thick and on aged trees it assumes pronounced ridges. Port Orford cedar grows slowly and can live for 600 years. It is known worldwide in the nursery trade with over 150 ornamental varieties bred from it. Most of these only remotely resemble the form of a mature, close-grown forest tree.

Tulip tree

Liriodendron tulipifera

The tallest deciduous broadleaf tree of the temperate forests of the world is the black cottonwood, described earlier, which grows along the Pacific coast of North America. The second tallest is a product of the expansive hardwood forests of the eastern section of this continent. The tulip tree, known in the lumber trade as yellow poplar, is not only an exceptionally tall tree but also has other fine qualities that make it stand out even in the midst of one of the greatest assemblages of superb trees ever produced in the temperate realms of this planet.

When it grows in a forest its great span of foliage is upheld by a fluted, straight, cylindrical bole that may be clear of branches for 30 metres (100 feet) from the

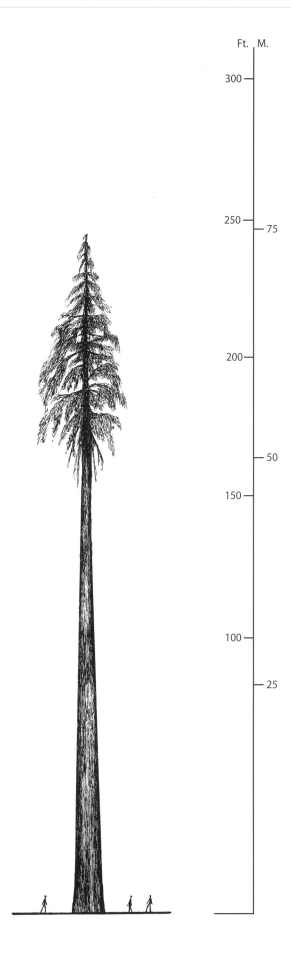

Figure 14: **Port Orford cedar**,
Chamaecyparis lawsoniana

*The largest specimen of Port Orford
cedar stood on a slope of the Upper
Coquille River, Oregon. It was 5.2
metres (17 feet) thick at the top of its
3.7-metre (12-foot) stump. After felling
it was found to be 74.7 metres (245
feet) long.*

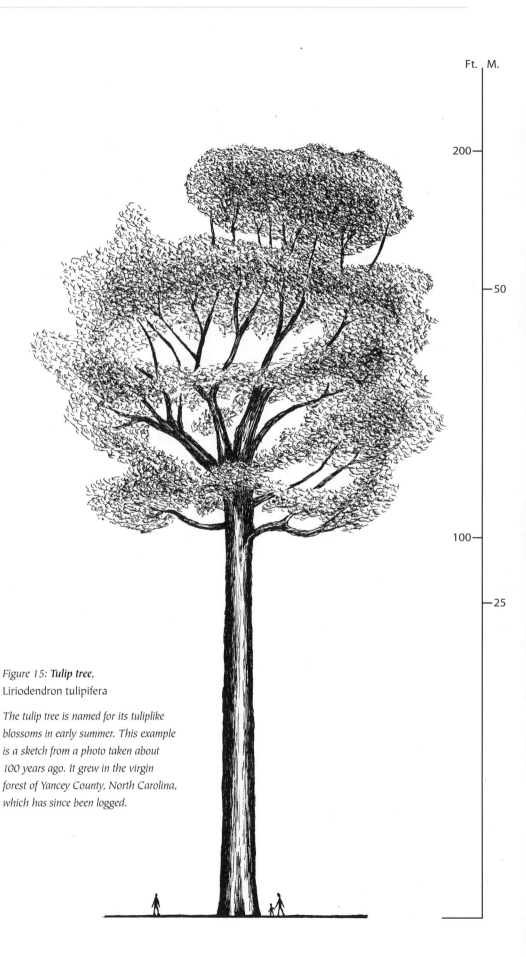

Ft. M.

200

50

100

25

Figure 15: **Tulip tree**,
Liriodendron tulipifera

The tulip tree is named for its tuliplike
blossoms in early summer. This example
is a sketch from a photo taken about
100 years ago. It grew in the virgin
forest of Yancey County, North Carolina,
which has since been logged.

ground[99] (note Figure 15). In the open, the lower branches are retained and the tree takes on a different aspect, but still has a towering and most imposing form, beautifully foliaged with glossy saddle-shaped leaves that are intermixed in early summer with tuliplike flowers. Those who know the eastern North American forest intimately say that a more stately tree does not exist.[100]

A comparison of the height of these two champions of stature, the giant of the eastern forests and the western cottonwood, is of interest, though they are in no way related. The tallest tulip tree ever measured almost touched 55 metres (180 feet),[101] while a cottonwood was recorded at 70.1 metres (230 feet).[102] Both species have sizeable trunks. The cottonwood excels with a bole 3.8 metres (12.4 feet) thick at a man's breast height,[103] while the greatest measured diameter at this point for the tulip tree is 3.7 metres (12.1 feet).[104] The tulip tree, however, has a more expansive crown, usually about a third greater in width than that of the cottonwood. Moreover, it is more substantially built, giving a maximum lifespan of 600 years compared to 250 for the cottonwood.[105] The leaves of both turn a beautiful golden yellow in the autumn, enhancing their value as ornamental trees for large parks or broad streets.

The tree presented in Figure 15 is a sketch from a photo taken about 100 years ago. It grew in the virgin forest of Yancey County, North Carolina. It did not stand alone, as the photo shows others in the background which appear to be of equal size.[106] These trees were logged out, of course, as the tulip tree affords valued lumber.

The above account deals only with the maxima. Such trees are extremely rare. Mature tulip trees, healthy and vigorous in favoured localities of deep, rich soil, generally reach 30.5 to 45.7 metres (100 to 150 feet) high with boles 1.5 to 1.8 metres (5 to 6 feet) thick. The finest trees are found in the lower Ohio River Valley, such as in Indiana, and also in sheltered recesses of the southern Appalachian Mountains, such as in North Carolina.

Tule Tree

Taxodium mucronatum

The giant and ancient tree at Tule, Oaxaca State, Mexico, is an amazing creation, millennia old and still possessing a full head of foliage, but most spectacular is its width of trunk—11.6 metres (38 feet) at a man's breast height (Figure 16).[107]

The Tule tree is of the species Montezuma baldcypress, *Taxodium mucronatum*. It is almost exclusively indigenous to Mexico, and many giant specimens are to be found there. Some are taller but none has such a great domelike spread of foliage or such an expansive trunk. It is not tall—only 42.7 metres (140 feet)—but the span of its crown is 45.7 metres (150 feet). At about 9 metres (30 feet) from the ground the

*Figure 16: **Tule Tree***

The Montezuma cypress is almost exclusively indigenous to Mexico, and many giant specimens are found there. The giant and ancient tree at Tule, Oaxaca State, Mexico, is millennia old and still possesses a full head of foliage, but most spectacular is the width of its trunk: 11.6 metres (38 feet) at breast height.

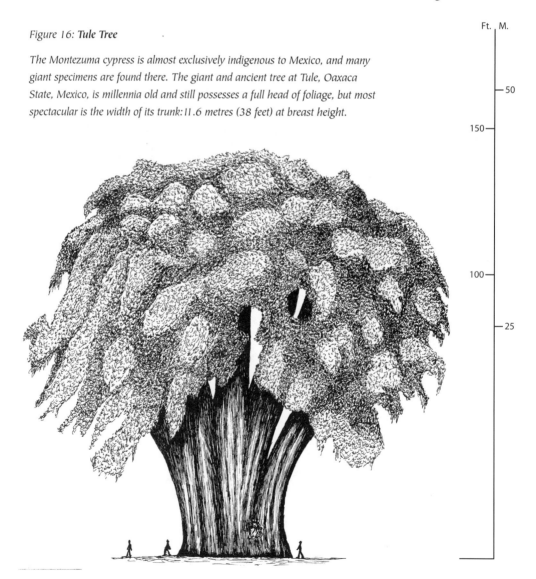

trunk divides into several huge branches that expand outward. It can be argued that the Tule Tree has the greatest thickness of trunk of any living tree in the world. The only other contender seems to be the baobab tree, *Adansonia digitata*, in Africa, where there is the rare specimen that rivals the Tule Tree. The trunks of the giant sequoias, *Sequoiadendron giganteum*, of California, although much taller, are less in diameter. A chestnut tree, *Castanea sativa*, on the slope of Mount Etna, on the Mediterranean island of Sicily, at one time had a greater thickness of trunk but is now but a relic. (Note Chart 3, p. 138.)

The Tule Tree appears to be of great age, and extensive research shows it has had a long and remarkable history. It was an outstanding tree when the Spaniards first reported on it in 1586, over 410 years ago. The local inhabitants say it was hit by lightning long before that, and before then it was a mighty tree, big enough to shade a thousand men.[108] The lightning strike blasted it from the top to the very heart, leaving it hollow and split into several pieces. These gradually grew and fused, perhaps over a period of 500 years.

In 1630, or 375 years ago, the tree was viewed by a traveller, Bernabe Cobo. At that time it consisted of several parts. There were three openings large enough to be entered by a man on a horse, and the hollow was some 4.6 metres (15 feet) in diameter, big enough to accommodate 12 horsemen. The outside diameter was about 7.6 metres (25 feet).[109] By 1766, or some 230 years ago, the hollow had been closed over by new growth or at least could not be seen from the outside. The trunk then had a diameter of 41 feet (12.5 metres). This was apparently based on a perimeter where the trunk's sinuosities, that is, its in-curves and out-curves, were taken into account. By 1840 the hollow could only be perceived by climbing into the main branches of the tree and looking down.[110]

For a long time people questioned whether the Tule Tree was always a single tree or if it was a fusion of several trees. Some of the different botanists who have examined it over the years declare it to have always been one tree, while others claim that it is composed of at least three trees that coalesced over time. Recent testing has shown that all parts of the tree indicate genetic uniformity, proving that it was always one tree.[111]

The age of this gargantuan tree is unknown. It is usually given as 2,000 years, but 3,000 would seem a truer estimate.[112]

EUROPE

English oak

Quercus robur

Linnaeus could not have selected a better word than "*robur*" for the species name of this tree. "*Robur*" is Latin for pure ruggedness. The late Alan Mitchell, England's noted tree expert, used the term "rugged robustitude" to describe it. This tree is attacked by more kinds of insects and fungi than any other, yet thrives remarkably well. It can endure rot for hundreds of years without succumbing. Trees of English oak, *Quercus robur*, have been known to be struck by lightning from top to bottom and live for centuries after. Others have hollow trunks caused by rot, with cavities big enough for one to walk into, turn around in a circle and walk out, then find that this very act was done by people a century earlier in the same tree. Yet the tree stands fully decked in verdure. *Robur*, then, is a perfectly descriptive word, but what about "English"? This apparently is ideal, too, even though this oak is indigenous to most parts of Europe and eastward into the borderlands of southwestern Asia, and south across the Mediterranean to the northwestern fringe of Africa. It is, however, inalienably associated with the history of England in that the country's navy of oaken ships built an Empire. It is also referred to as the "common" oak because of its wide natural distribution in Europe and adjoining regions.

English or common oak is a stalwart tree (Figure 17). When fully mature it supports a wide-spreading crown that seems to defy gravity. It is not as tall as many other species of oak. The bole supporting the giant framework of branches, however, is enormous. The tree with the thickest bole in England is usually given as the Bowthorpe Oak near the town of Bourne, Lincolnshire. Most recent measurements show it to have a breast-height trunk diameter of 4.1 metres (13.4 feet). This tree has an expansive hollow, 1.8 by 2.7 metres (6 by 9 feet), and from all accounts it has had this for over a century as 50 years ago even the most ancient old-timers of the nearby countryside could not remember when it was otherwise. Nevertheless, it is showing its age as its expansion of trunk is very slow. It is thought to be at least 1,000 years old.[113] Alan Mitchell was of the opinion, based on his hundreds of measurements of oak trees at all stages of development, that for an English oak to attain a trunk girth of 12.2 metres (40 feet), corresponding to a diameter of 3.9 metres (12.7 feet), it would have to be about 1,000 years old.

A much younger tree, the Majesty Oak near Fredville, Kent, is thought on good evidence to be about 480 years old. It is growing faster than the Bowthorpe Oak and in a few decades it will probably surpass it in size. It is a more handsome tree, taller and more vigorous, but it, too, is hollow, though only narrowly. Still, one can look up its vent and see the blue of the sky 9 metres (30 feet) above. Its trunk is 3.8 metres (12.6 feet) in diameter at breast height.[114]

Most of these very ancient oaks, such as that at Bowthorpe, are pollarded. This means that at some time during their history their crown limbs were cut off above the height where deer and cattle would browse on them. Such wood was used for structural purposes or for firewood. It is not certain if the Fredville tree is a pollard. It may be what is termed a maiden or unpollarded tree. Pollarded trees do seem to live longer than those not so treated. When a tree is pollarded it produces multiple heads, so when one head dies the tree is better able to carry on.

The Marton Oak in the county of Cheshire, England, is split into two widely separated parts, but each supports healthy branches with canopies. Careful measurement has shown that the trunk of this tree has a breast-height diameter of 4.3 metres (14.0 feet), making it larger than the Bowthorpe Oak. There is therefore some justification for the claim that it is the largest living oak in the British Isles, at least from the standpoint of trunk size.[115]

Until it was struck by lightning in 1956, the Newland Oak in Gloucestershire was for years the undisputed champion oak in England. It had a bole 4.45 metres (14.6

*Figure 17: **English oak**, Quercus robur*

England is blessed with two great and rugged oak species: the English or common oak and its cousin, the sessile oak, sometimes referred to as the durmast oak. The English oak is predominately found in the lowlands of mid- and southern England, and the sessile is chiefly found in the higher and more mountainous sections to the west and north. The two interbreed so there are many hybrids.

feet) in diameter at breast height. At the time lightning delivered its fatal blow it was a complete tree with a full head of branches. Old photographs show it to be indeed a monster. Its remains can still be seen.[116]

Measurements made in 1820 on the Winfarthing Oak in Norfolk, England, showed it to be 3.9 metres (12.7 feet) in diameter at breast height. Its shell could easily hold 30 men and at one time meetings were conducted therein. The tree did not completely collapse until 1953.[117]

Going back further into history, records show that there were some mighty oaks, but just how big they were according to today's method of measuring is difficult to say. One ancient giant was the Cowthorpe Oak in the Nidd Valley of Yorkshire. This tree, which was bearing acorns in 1864, collapsed before 1900. Its remnants can still be seen. It was measured by John Evelyn about 1660 and its trunk then had a diameter of 4.7 metres (15.3 feet) at 0.9 metres (3 feet) above the ground. An excellent engraving of it shows its trunk to have a rather marked taper, so the measurement would be somewhat less at breast height.[118]

England is blessed with two great and rugged oak species that followed upon the retreat of the ice age some 7,000 years ago. Both are extremely hardy and can live to an immense age. The English or common oak, described above, is also referred to as the pedunculate oak because its acorns are suspended on definite stalks or peduncles. The acorns of its cousin, the sessile oak, adhere without stalks, as its name implies, to the fruiting twig. The sessile is sometimes referred to as the durmast oak. The English oak is predominately a tree of the lowlands of mid- and southern England, while the sessile is chiefly found in the higher and more mountainous sections to the west and north. These oaks interbreed so there are many hybrids. The two species are alike in so many ways that they are not given individual treatment here.

The sessile oak, *Quercus petraea*, has its ancient giants. It is generally a taller oak than the English kind, but its branches are not so wide spreading. Its bole on occasion extends quite high free of branches. Trees with boles 18.3 to 19.8 metres (60 to 65 feet) clear have been found. The tallest of the two oaks in England is a sessile at 43.9 metres (144 feet), while the English species' record is 42.1 metres (138 feet). About 1900 a sessile oak was found in the Belleme Forest, Normandy, France, that was 44.5 metres (146 feet) tall with a clear bole of 34.5 metres (113 feet).[119]

There are two very ancient and immensely large sessile oaks in England. One, the Queen Elizabeth Oak in Cowdray Park, Sussex, is very hollow and thought to be close to 1,000 years old. It is said that in 1573 Queen Elizabeth had her entourage make a detour so that she could view the giant tree. It now has a bole 4 metres (13.1 feet) in diameter at breast height. It is a pollarded oak.[120] The other outstandingly ancient and large sessile oak is the Lydham Manor Oak in Shropshire. It is estimated to be 700 years old, is a pollard and is growing at a good rate for an old tree. Its trunk is 3.8 metres (12.5 feet) thick at breast height. Growing from its huge, burled bole are other trees such as holly and elder.[121]

English or sessile, the biggest girthed oak in England was the gigantic specimen that at one time stood near Hempstead, Essex. It was measured before it was destroyed and was found to be 5.2 metres (16.9 feet) in diameter of trunk at the slimmest point. There are no reports on it after about 1870.[122]

Although the British Isles are well supplied with big and ancient trees, every country in continental Europe has its quota, especially France and Germany. One of the largest and most magnificent oaks in France is the Chêne de Tronjoli, a common or English oak. It is a handsome giant with a fine head of foliage. Its bole is 3.9 metres (12.7 feet) in diameter at breast height, hollow and slightly split. It is thought to be nearly 1,000 years old.[123] There is a famous tree near the town of Yvetot, Normandy, named the Allouville-Bellfosse Oak. Its hollow bole is 3.8 metres (12.5 feet) thick, and two chapels have been cut in it, one above the other. The age of this tree is in question, but it is thought to be over 1,000 years old. It has been a place of devotion for 300 years.[124]

What is believed to be the largest and oldest oak in Germany is the Feme Eiche or Trial Oak at Erle, a village near the town of Raesfeld, Westphalia. In times past, public meetings or trials were held beneath it. It is a squat tree and much decayed. The bole is 3.7 metres (12 feet) thick at breast height and it is estimated to be 1,500 years old, but this may be apocryphal.[125]

Near the town of Ivenack, 130 kilometres (80 miles) north of Berlin, is a grove of majestic oaks, all in a rugged state of health. The largest of these is outstandingly admirable. Its bole is 3.7 metres (12 feet) thick at breast height and solid, with no branches for 7.6 metres (25 feet). It could be the largest well-preserved oak in Europe and it rivals those in England. A sign nearby says it is 1,200 years old.[126] These oaks, like that at Erle, are of the common or English kind. The oak with the greatest width of trunk at breast height is at Kvill in Sweden, and it is known as the Kvillehen. At this height its trunk is 4.8 metres (15.9 feet) in diameter, but it has a pronounced taper so it is much less where the branches begin at about 3 metres (10 feet) up.[127]

The Methuselah of all oaks seems to be one known as the Kongeegan or King's Oak in the Forest of Nordskoven, Denmark. It is a hulk with a few leafy branches. The trunk is wide open and severely eroded. It must have been at one time over 3.7 metres (12 feet) in diameter at breast height. It is said to be 2,000 years old and has certainly experienced well over 1,000 years. It is a common oak.[128]

Did larger oaks than now exist once stand in continental Europe? In France 100 years ago a gigantic oak called the Chêne de Mon Travail stood near the village of Pessines in the Charentes region. It was hollow, and inside was fashioned a little room about 3.7 metres (12 feet) wide equipped with a semicircular bench carved from the wood of the tree. From the descriptions then given, this tree was something out of the ordinary, a behemoth. It was well known and travellers came from afar to view it. Dr. Kanngiesser, a German botanist, visited it in 1906 and his measurements showed that its trunk was 4.6 metres (15 feet) thick at breast height. It still stands but is little more than a remnant.[129]

Another oak, famous in times past, was near the town of Belfort, eastern France. It was called the Chêne Sans Pareil (or Nonpareil) and was felled in 1858. It measured 4.1 metres (13.4 feet) where cut across near breast height. This and the oak near Pessines were said to be about 2,000 years old, but there seems no substantiation for such claims. Both are of the English or common kind.[130]

Sweet chestnut

Castanea sativa

ere is a tree imbued with the ability to keep sprouting new growth after it is long past maturity and even in the throes of old age. In doing so, root and stem seemingly expand forever. Finally the trunk may assume a Brobdingnagian size.

A sweet chestnut tree on the east slope of volcanic Mount Etna, on the island of Sicily, some 550 metres (1,800 feet) above the sea clearly exemplifies this ability. There are many other huge sweet chestnut trees in this area. Some are taller but none has the vast expanse of bole. This tree became famous several centuries ago when in 1380, Joan, Queen of Aragon, on her way to view Mount Etna, was caught by a sudden storm and took refuge beneath the tree along with her escort of 100 horsemen. From that time on the tree was known at the *Castagno di Cento Cavalli*, or Chestnut Tree of 100 Horses.[131]

This tree became well known and, as the years passed, people interested in the wonders of nature would come to view it. The traveller Kircher paid a visit in 1670. He described it as a huge hollow tree whose cavity was serving as a corral for a flock of sheep. The next visitor was Houel, in about 1700, who found a house and kiln for drying the nuts from the tree within the centre space. The first recorded measurement of the tree was made by Brydone in 1770. He found the trunk to be 62.2 metres (204 feet) in girth or 19.8 metres (65 feet) in diameter. It was again measured by Count Borch in 1780, who reported 57.9 metres (190 feet) in girth or 18.4 metres (60.5 feet) in diameter.[132] By 1865 the tree had split into five parts, all thriving. About this time several investigations were conducted to determine whether the tree—or trees—consisted of a single organism or of a group. By digging around the base it was found that all arose from a common footing or root.[133] When Luigi Scaccabarozzi, a tree enthusiast, visited the tree in 1990 there were only three well-separated sections left. The space between them varied from 3.7 to 4.6 metres (12 to 15 feet). The two largest pieces were about 5.5 metres (18 feet) in diameter at a few feet from the ground. One was hollow and the other had a double split. The total height of the foliage was about 21.3 metres (70 feet).[134]

Time has doubtless wrought some degradation on this tree, but much can be blamed on the activities of man. The nuts were greatly relished and a kiln was provided to dry them; fuel for this was hacked from the tree. During its long history it was used as a sheepfold and as a home. In later years tourists would break or cut off pieces for souvenirs.

Even in its prime the Chestnut Tree of 100 Horses was not tall, perhaps never more than 24.4 metres (80 feet). It was its colossal trunk that drew people's attention (Figure 18). We can only guess how old this tree is. It was obviously an enormous tree at the time of Joan of Aragon's visit over 600 years ago, and there are reports of it back to the time Plato lived in nearby Syracuse, some 2,300 years ago, so it was drawing attention even then. It may be 2,500 to 3,000 years old.[135]

There are reports of several other huge sweet chestnut trees in southern Europe. Some have passed into history, while others still stand. The largest is known as the Green Lizard chestnut and is located at Grisolia, in Cosenza province, northern Calabria, in the south of Italy. Its trunk is 4.4 metres (14.3 feet) thick at a man's breast height. It is a survivor, along with two lesser chestnut trees, of a grove of such trees.[136] Another tree of this species, almost as big, is at Capranica Prenestina, a village some 32 kilometres (20 miles) east of Rome.[137]

Two huge sweet chestnut trees in France are not significantly smaller than the giants of Italy, now that the Mount Etna tree has degenerated. One is in Brittany, south of the town of Quimper, and the other is far to the east, on the south shore of Lake Geneva (Lac Leman), about 12 kilometres (8 miles) east of the town of Thonon-les-Bains. Both trees have the stamp of great age. The Brittany tree, with a breast-height diameter of 4.2 metres (13.7 feet), may well have the thickest bole in France. It is reputed to be 1,000 years old. The Thonon tree is said to have sheltered a hermitage in 1408, indicating that even then it was of considerable size.[138]

The tallest sweet chestnut tree of which there is firm record was on the island of Madeira. It was a most majestic specimen, 48.8 metres (160 feet) high with a bole 3.7 metres (12.3 feet) in diameter. It was burned down in 1903.[139]

There is a famous tree in England, in Gloucestershire: the Tortworth Chestnut. It is not possible to obtain an accurate measurement because the many contortions,

*Figure 18: **Sweet chestnut**, Castanea sativa*

In 1380, Joan, Queen of Aragon, on her way to view Mount Etna, was caught by a sudden storm and took refuge beneath this tree along with her escort of 100 horsemen. From that time on the tree was known at the Castagno di Cento Cavalli, or Chestnut Tree of 100 Horses.

eruptions of new growth, decay of old sections, cavities, burls and sprouts confuse the issue. Some of the lower great branches have rotted and fallen away over the years, seemingly reducing its size. The latest measurements give the original trunk a width of 3.5 metres (11.5 feet), although 300 years ago the width was as much as 5.5 metres (18.2 feet). Again we can only guess at this tree's age. It has been suggested that it was planted by the Romans, who first brought the nuts to England, but there is no evidence to substantiate this fact. One investigator has dated its planting to the time of King Egbert, 1,200 years ago; others to a somewhat later date.[140] It must have been a notable tree in the time of King John, 800 years ago, as it was then described as the "Great or Old Chestnut Tree at Tortworth," with a crown span of 57.3 metres (188 feet).[141] It has been claimed to be the oldest living tree in Britain, but this is not true, as many yew trees predate the coming of the Romans by at least a millennium and perhaps several (see p. below).

The Canford Chestnut, Canford School, Dorset, with a trunk 4.3 metres (14.2 feet) thick has good grounds to be acclaimed the tree with the greatest width of solid bole of any in the British Isles.[142]

Common, European or English yew

Taxus baccata

> *O not for thee the glow, the bloom,*
> *Who changest not in any gale,*
> *Nor branding summer suns avail*
> *To touch thy thousand years of gloom.*

—Alfred Lord Tennyson, 1850

Using conjecture based on historical evidence, it would seem that the most ancient tree living in the world today is the Fortingall Yew in Perthshire, Scotland. We cannot obtain proof of the tree's age as its core wood rotted away centuries, perhaps millennia ago, leaving no growth rings to count nor any first-formed wood or like substance for carbon-14 analysis. Instead of using these methods, we must rely on the tree's trunk size.

Hundreds of measurements of ancient yews, combined with historical evidence, have shown that when a yew tree has gained a trunk close to 3.7 metres (12 feet) in diameter, it is around 5,000 years old.[143] Most of the annual growth rings are in the

Figure 19: **Common**, **European** *or* **English yew**, Taxus baccata

The Brabourne Yew in Kent, England, in the grounds of the Church of St. Mary the Virgin was found to have a circumference of 17.8 metres (58.5 feet) or a diameter of 5.7 metres (18.6 feet) in 1650. A search was made for it in 1889 but there was no vestige left.

outer half of the diameter, as the rate of growth decelerates as the tree ages. The belief that the Fortingall Yew is 7,000 years old is based on its trunk size, which is quite extraordinary.[144]

The Fortingall Yew is now a relic, although a healthy one, and its bole dimensions cannot be determined accurately, but this was possible over a century ago. In 1890 an assiduously conducted measurement showed it to have a trunk 15.9 metres (52 feet) in girth or 5.1 metres (16.6 feet) in diameter.[145] The conjecture is, if a tree with a bole 3.7 metres in diameter is 5,000 years old, how old is the Fortingall Yew, with a bole over one third as large again?

The Fortingall Yew was not the only outsized yew in the British Isles in times past. In 1650 there stood the Brabourne Yew in Kent, England, in the grounds of the Church of St. Mary the Virgin (Figure 19). Like the Fortingall, it was a churchyard tree. John Evelyn says he measured its trunk at near 6.1 metres (20 feet) in diameter, but adds that it was measured at the time more exactly by order of the Right Hon. Sir George Carteret, vice-chamberlain to His Majesty, and found to have a circumference of 17.8 metres (58.5 feet) or a diameter of 5.7 metres (18.6 feet).[146] No mention is made of how far up the trunk this measurement was taken, but this information is not too significant for yews as they rise more or less vertically. Some time after this event the tree disappeared, probably a victim of development. A search was made for it in 1889 but there was no vestige left. Its measurement showed it vaster than the Fortingall Yew and it was well known in Evelyn's time and was reported on by others.[147]

Measurements made on ancient churchyard yews in England show many with trunk girths of 9.1 to 12.2 metres (30 to 40 feet) which would yield diameters of 2.9 to 3.9 metres (9.6 to 12.7 feet). Research on these trees indicates that those with a trunk thickness of 3.2 metres (10.5 feet) are about 3,000 years old, while those 3.5 metres (11.5 feet) thick are approaching 5,000 years of age. All the measurements indicate that the trunk diameter of such ancient yews increases less than 1.27 centimetres (0.5 inch) in one hundred years. Sometimes the growth is so small as to be unmeasurable. Some of the oldest have been confirmed to have occupied ancient burial sites as far back as the Neolithic or late Stone Age, 3,000 to 5,000 years ago.[148]

Most of the largest yews stand next to churches and it was at one time thought that they were planted at the time the church was founded, even perhaps in early medieval times, A.D. 700 to 800. It is now known that in most cases the yew antedated the establishment of the church and in fact may have been centuries and even millennia old at that time.[149]

The common, European or English yew seems to be one tree that in some instances can live forever. Certain very ancient specimens possess the ability to form sprouts that descend from the living tree, root and establish new wood while older parts of the tree rot and disintegrate. In this way whole new trees have formed within or as part of the original structure.[150]

The slowness of the growth of ancient yews has been mentioned. Alan Mitchell, Britain's tree expert, found that sometimes he could discern no increase in the girth or diameter of bole over a period of 20 years.[151] An outstanding example of this is the Totteridge Yew in Hertfordshire. Its bole was first measured in 1677 at 0.9 metres (3 feet) above the ground. It then had a diameter of 2.52 metres (8.28 feet). It was measured again at the same distance from the ground twice in the 1700s, once in the 1800s and twice in the mid- to late 1900s. In all this time the measurements remained the same, indicating that the tree's bole had not changed in girth or diameter in over 300 years. Despite this, the tree remains perfectly healthy in every respect.[152] Normally yew trees do expand in girth, however slowly, and measurements show that the Crowhurst Yew in Sussex increased its diameter of bole 26.9 centimetres (10.6 inches) in 318 years.[153]

Long before the world was blessed with Christianity and its places of religious intent were founded, the yew tree was venerated by humans, possibly because they noticed that it was always green, was changed little by the fiercest gale and remained much the same in a human lifetime, indeed in several lifetimes. It thus assumed an aura of immortality. Old trees grow exceedingly slowly and their boles assume a marked fluted appearance, an insignia of age. The interior wood rots away and the tree becomes a shell, sometimes split with an opening sufficiently wide to permit passage inside. The cavity of certain trees, such as that at Much Marcle, Herefordshire, has been fitted with seats with room enough for 12 people.[154] In general the profile of a yew tree is usually quite squat, even when it has developed a considerable expanse of bole, which may extend upward 3 metres (10 feet). Full height of tree is 12 to 18 metres (40 to 60 feet), although the exceptional specimen may reach to 29 metres (95 feet). The crown span can be considerable. A tree in east Lothian, Scotland, has a mean spread of foliage of

35 metres (115 feet). The bark of mature trees is a deep reddish brown, can be peeled in flaky strips and is less than 2.5 centimetres (1 inch) thick. The leaves are needlelike and the fruit is an aril, a bright red, succulent, berrylike nodule. The yew is, of course, a conifer but of an ancient lineage, much more ancient than those that bear cones.

The common yew grows natively over most of Europe, especially the central and southern parts. It can also be found along the fringe of northwest Africa and east through Turkey as far as the Caucasus Mountains. There are several ancient trees in France with expansive boles that rival those in England. One in the cemetery of Estry, Normandy, has a bole thickness of 3.6 metres (11.7 feet), while another in Normandy at La Haye de Routot is almost as large and contains a small chapel within its hollow.[155]

Of vast circumference and gloom profound
This solitary tree! a living thing
Produced too slowly ever to decay;
Of form and aspect too magnificent
To be destroyed.

—William Wordsworth, 1830

Oriental plane

Platanus orientalis

This is a book of facts, not fiction. Every effort has been made to screen out apocryphal material. This is difficult in the case of the oriental plane tree because there are few facts that prove colossal and ancient trees of this species existed or still exist, but there are many stories of such enormous trees. For example, legend has it that the tree under which Hippocrates (460–377 B.C.) sat and expounded his wisdom on human ailments still stands on the island of Cos in the Aegean Sea, but the evidence seems to indicate that what is left is a regeneration from its roots rather than the actual tree.[156] There is the report of the great king Xerxes of Persia, at the head of his army of over 300,000 men marching to invade Greece, calling a halt so that he might tarry a few days to sit under the shade and admire a grove of huge plane trees. This took place near the ancient city of Sardis, far from the sea, and the heat and drought of the country must have been wearisome. An oriental plane tree, even a moderate sized one, can be strikingly beautiful under such conditions, with its large, maple-like, bright and fresh green leaves, made more inviting by the contrasting light grey bark of its mighty limbs. There are also travellers' reports of the remains of vast trees that they came upon in Afghanistan and Tajikistan, far to the east of Turkey where Xerxes rested under his tree.

What throws the light of truth on these stories is that the Bujukere Tree on the Bosporus became well known nearly 1,000 years ago and was measured and reported on while still in its majestic state. It is now but a ruin. Its serious decline set in soon after the turn of the last century, about 1910, and this was caused by ditching nearby to facilitate drainage. However, long before this, in about 1090 at the time of the first Crusade, soldiers rested under its shade and descriptions of it filtered through to the western nations. It was further reported on during the following centuries and a drawing of it was made in the early years of the nineteenth century. About this time it was measured by two different men, both students of nature. Their measurements are in fair agreement. First, in about 1820 Augustin de Candolle found by measuring the circumference that the trunk of the tree had a basal diameter of 14.6 metres (47.8 feet) and the mean width of the huge hollow within was 8.6 metres (28.3 feet).[157] In 1831 it was measured by British forester Dr. Walsh, and its trunk then girthed 43 metres (141 feet) at the base, or 13.7 metres (44.9 feet) in diameter.[158]

*Figure 20: **Oriental plane**, Platanus orientalis*

There are many stories of enormous oriental plane trees, but few are as well-documented as the Bujukere Tree on the Bosporus, which became well known nearly 1,000 years ago. In about 1090 at the time of the first Crusade, soldiers rested under its shade and descriptions of it filtered through to the western nations. In 1831 its trunk measured 13.7 metres (44.9 feet) in diameter at the base.

Figure 20 is from a drawing of the Bujukere Tree before it entered serious decline. It was one of several plane trees close to the village of Bujukere near Constantinople, now Istanbul. We have indulged in a little artistic licence, in that the top has been restored to what it was when the tree was near its prime, since it is obvious that it had long passed this point when the original drawing was made.

Oriental plane trees are known to attain great size, occasionally 45.7 metres (150 feet) high with an equal canopy span. In the Mediterranean world and to the east, all the giant trees seem located near streams or a source of fresh water. There is a report of a tree in Armenia that has a height of 50 metres (164 feet) and a trunk diameter of 10 metres (32.8 feet).[159] There is little doubt, too, that the oriental plane could attain an immense age as well as size. In 1842 an imposing tree stood in the village of Vostiza on the Gulf of Lepanto, Greece, that was 42.7 metres (140 feet) high with a 3.7-metre (12-foot) diameter of trunk. This tree was said to have been planted by Menelaus, King of Sparta and husband of Helen of Troy, about 1125 B.C. It caught the eye of the highly regarded historian Pausanias, who did most of his travelling, investigating and writing between A.D. 143 and 176. He was very interested in natural phenomena and enthused over the beauty and size of the Vostiza Tree. It must have been 1,300 years old then. Henry Elwes, the outstanding chronicler of trees in the early years of the last century, tracked it down in 1904, by which time it was but a hollow stump. He says that the last vestiges of life faded away about 1900.[160] From these various reports it would seem that this tree lived for 3,200 years before it succumbed.

The oriental plane tree seems to have arisen in the region bordering the Aegean Sea whence it radiated out, sometimes helped by man, to the east through Turkey, Iraq, Iran, Afghanistan, Tajikistan and as far as Kashmir. Travellers report encountering sizeable trees in all these territories. There is an early traveller's account of a huge tree he came upon at Shodjakent, a village in the foothills of the Lshistchik Mountains, east of Tashkent. This tree had a main trunk that was hollow and part rotten, and six much smaller, living, lateral trunks protruded from its perimeter. The cavity of the main trunk had a diameter of 9 metres (30 feet).[161] One may think that this is a circumference figure, but it is not very different from the great hollow of the well-measured Bujukere Tree.

The Romans, who greatly admired the plane tree, were instrumental in spreading it to various parts of their empire, bringing it first to Sicily and what is now Italy in about 360 B.C. They also brought back descriptions of huge trees in Asia Minor. One report concerns Lucinis Mucianus, the consul of Lycia, holding a feast with 18 guests in the hollow of a plane tree.[162] Pliny (A.D. 23–79) described a plane tree, presumably the one in Lycia (southwest Turkey), that had a hollow 24.7 metres (81 feet) around or 7.9 metres (25.8 feet) in mean diameter. The walls, he said, were sheathed in places with moss, but the tree's crown was so verdant that it was largely impenetrable to the rays of the sun.[163]

Apparently these legends and half-legends about the enormous size and age of certain oriental plane trees have a basis of fact, so this world has undoubtedly witnessed trees of this species that have trunks over 13.7 metres (45 feet) thick and that have lived for well over 2,000 years.

SOUTHERN HEMISPHERE

Kauri

Agathis australis

The kauri of New Zealand is not only a giant but also a strange tree. Some of its features are unique. It can change its entire branch structure while developing. In its formative years it grows as a tall, spirelike tree, commonly called a ricker. This configuration is retained until it has reached above the general level of the surrounding vegetation. At this point the branching habit metamorphoses. A number of strong leading buds burst out from the terminal head of the central stem and grow sideways and upwards to form a huge, wide-spreading crown. Soon the original branches of the ricker atrophy and are sloughed off in a way that is similar to a deciduous tree dropping its leaves in autumn. The tree's bole is therefore largely free of knots and has little or no taper. As the substantial new branches extend, some added support is necessary, but this is not obtained by buttressing or fluting of the bole. Rather, large platelike knobs form among the major roots deep below the ground. After about 200 years the kauri has assumed its mature shape and may carry on for hundreds of years. A further innovation that it has is the constant shedding of flakes of bark. This discourages climbing vines and the attachment of epiphytes, so the tree retains a clear bole even in old age.

A kauri forest is a wondrous sight to walk through. Large, grey, well-spaced pillars support a continuous green canopy high above, producing an effect much like that inside a gothic cathedral, where the light is subdued and only an occasional shaft of the sun's rays breaks through. Small shrubs, ferns and kauri grass, *Astelia trinervia*, cover the forest floor.

Of living trees, the greatest is known as the Tane Mahuta, or Lord of the Forest. The dimensions of this tree are: total height 51.5 metres (169 feet); length of trunk clear of branches 17.7 metres (58 feet); diameter of trunk 4.4 metres (14.4 feet); estimated age 2,100 years.[164] Like all ancient kauris, its trunk is hollow. This tree is showing its age but will likely stand for centuries yet if protected. Another giant, Te Matua Ngahere, or Father of the Forest, has a thicker trunk with a diameter of 5.1 metres (16.6 feet) but is a squatter tree. Both trees are in the Waipoua Forest Sanctuary. There are several other huge specimens in this forest, but all are in various respects less in size.

Greater trees than Tane Mahuta are known to have existed before the destruction wrought by the Europeans. Some of these trees were so majestic and awesome that there were instances when the timber people's curiosity overcame their avarice and the trees were measured, at least in part. They were then, of course, chopped down. The biggest well-recorded tree was the great Kairaru in the Tutemoe Forest, a few miles south of the Waipoua. This tree did not fall victim to the timberman's axe but was consumed by fire late in the 1890s. Fires were not only due to the logger's inroads but also to land clearing by settlers. The Kairaru dwarfed the Tane Mahuta. Its bole, like that of all kauri trees, had little or no taper and extended upward for 30.5 metres (100 feet). It was 6.4 metres (21 feet) thick (note Figure 21). Its volume of commercial timber was estimated at 889 cubic metres (31,415 cubic feet) compared to 249 cubic metres (8,794 cubic feet) for that of the Tane Mahuta.[165] Indeed, the Kairaru rivalled the greatest of the California redwoods in timber production.

There were trees measured that had a thicker bole than the Kairaru but were squat. The Mercury Bay Kauri had a trunk 7.3 metres (23.9 feet) thick that was clear of branches for 24.4 metres (80 feet). This tree was destroyed by lightning in the 1850s. There are records of trees that had a greater width of trunk than even the Mercury Bay Kauri. One in the Coromandel Range was reputed to have a diameter of 8.5 metres (28 feet). This tree was well known locally during the 1860s and '70s, but just what its fate was seems uncertain. One huge tree had a clear bole length of 39.6 metres (130 feet) with a width of 5 metres (16.4 feet), all solid timber. This truly magnificent tree was felled for lumber, probably with little scruple. One tree that was felled for a spar had a clean bole for 45.7 metres (150 feet).[166]

Just what height the kauri can attain seems never to have been resolved. The tallest tree standing is 56.4 metres (185 feet) high, but before the forests were ravaged by the Europeans there were undoubtedly taller trees. Early records give heights as great as 75 metres (246 feet), but these have never been verified. However, trees with clear boles 39.6 to 45.7 metres (130 to 150 feet) long must have been a good height, at least 61 metres (200 feet) or somewhat more, as the upward thrust of the crown is quite extensive—on average very nearly 30.5 metres (100 feet). Moreover, measurements show that trees with long boles do not necessarily have crowns of reduced size.[167]

The maximum age a kauri can attain is considered to be at least 4,000 years. The Tane Mahuta is estimated to be 2,100 years old, but larger trees such as the Mercury Bay Kauri would conceivably be much older. The wood of the stump of one giant tree, Kopi, which stood in the Omahuta Forest, was estimated by radiocarbon dating to have aged 4,000 years.[168]

The kauri, a masterpiece of nature, has undoubtedly suffered more than any other tree species from the greed of industrial man. When Captain Cook returned from his initial voyage to New Zealand, 1768–71, he reported viewing trees taller, straighter and finer than any he had ever seen. The irony of it was that Cook never viewed a kauri tree. Neither did the botanists, Sir Joseph Banks and Dr. Daniel Solander, who accompanied him. They were looking at the ranks of another tree, kahikatea (white pine), *Dacrycarpus dacrydioides*, that bordered the river up which they journeyed[169] (see p. 69). It was not long before ships stopped there for spars to refit their masts, and then soon after for timber, much of which was kauri. Thus erupted one of the

*Figure 21: **Kauri**, Agathis australis*

The kauri of New Zealand was valued not only for timber but also for resin and was consequently nearly wiped from the face of the earth by the ship building trade.

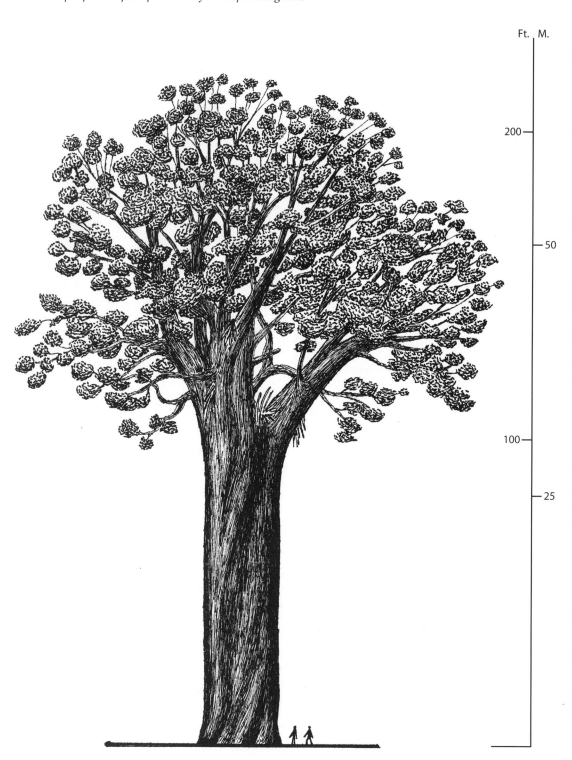

most wanton assaults ever made on a forest, not only for timber but also for the gum or resin that the tree produced. Trees were bled until they were anemic to satisfy the builders' trade. Greed pushed by competition knows no bounds. The giant kauri trees were almost wiped from the face of the earth before, finally, the altruistic sense of man came to the fore. There is now Tane Mahuta and some dozen other giant trees left—a monument of love for something other than money!

A mystery shrouds the kauri tree. It has a long history extending back 200 million years. As we have seen, over that time it has evolved some superior ways of successfully holding its own in the natural world, but despite these innovations it never achieved more than a toehold on New Zealand. It is confined to a tract of country north of the 38th parallel of latitude. The reason may be that it first came into being as a subtropical organism and cannot successfully compete with the vegetation types that thrive where cooler temperatures prevail.

Kahikatea (white pine)

Dacrycarpus dacrydioides

This is one of the most widespread trees of New Zealand. It was the forest of this species that aroused the attention of Captain Cook and his botanists, Sir Joseph Banks and Dr. Daniel Solander, on Cook's first visit in 1769. When they first sailed, and then rowed, up a river on the North Island, which Cook named the Thames (now the Waihou), they were astounded to see the dense forests lining the shores. Banks exclaimed that the trees were the tallest and slimmest he had ever seen. He noticed that their trunks extended a long way up with little taper before branching out. Kahikatea does at present represent the tallest native tree in New Zealand, approaching 61 metres (200 feet) in height.[170]

On well-watered or swampy lands where kahikateas especially thrive, they grow very tall. It is puzzling that on one hand their trunks have acquired some features to sustain their great height, such as fluting and moderate buttressing, but their timber is not strong and is not adapted to strain. They appeared to Captain Cook and his men ideal for ships' masts, so they took a quantity along for this purpose. The experiment failed as it was found they snapped too readily under stress.

Trees with trunks clear of branches for 27.4 metres (90 feet) have been measured. The thickest at breast height is 2.6 metres (8.6 feet) but on average they are much less

*Figure 22: **Kahikatea (white pine)**, Dacrycarpus dacrydioides*

A tall forest of kahikatea aroused the attention of Captain Cook on his first expedition to New Zealand in 1769. To Captain Cook and his men they appeared ideal for ships' masts, so they took a quantity along for this purpose. The experiment failed as it was found the timber snapped too readily under stress.

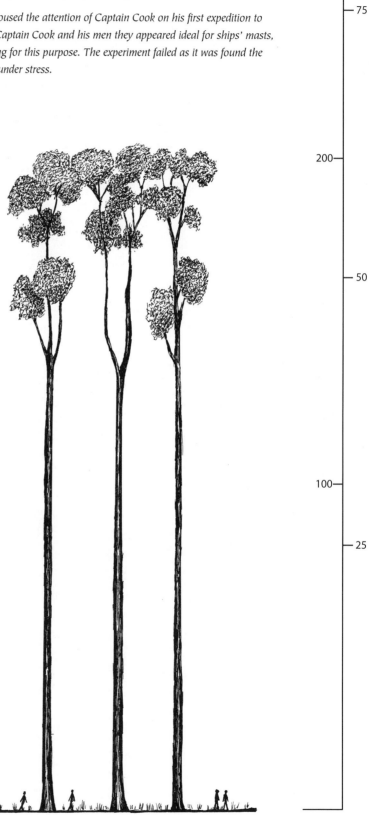

Ft. M.

— 75

200—

— 50

100—

— 25

than this. The trunks of mature trees are markedly fluted and splay out prominently near the ground. The bark is a pale grey and is shed continuously in ovoid flakes. It is thought that the tree can live for a very long time, even more than 2,000 years.[171] One peculiarity is that as kahikatea develops, it changes shape quite markedly. As a seedling it is a whiskery, straggly little tree up to about a metre (3 or 4 feet) high. Later, in the sapling stage, it forms a narrow conical crown and reaches up rapidly. At maturity it branches out strongly to a distance determined by the closeness of its neighbours. The leaf shape also changes as the tree develops. When young, the leaves are mostly of the juvenile form, resembling those of a yew tree. Later, when the tree is more fully grown, the leaves tend to the adult form, scalelike and more or less appressed to the stem.

In the wild, kahikatea flourishes with sparse and compact crowns in thick stands, but in isolation it branches out and forms a rather broad substantial head. Trees set apart by land clearing or logging become sentinels in pastures or in scrub and may stand out picturesquely. Some of them are well known.

Figure 22 is of three trees at the edge of a road near Lake Kaniere, on the west coast of South Island. At the time of my visit, there was a whole forest of these fully mature trees, crowded much closer together than shown here. Note the slender trunks clear of branches to great height, and also the terrain with swamp grass.

Fossil evidence suggests that kahikatea has a long ancestry. It can be traced back 35 to 50 million years, and its earliest progenitors go back long before this, possibly originating on the long-ago continent of Gondwanaland some 110 million years ago.[172]

Mountain ash

Eucalyptus regnans

> *Yes, you lie there in state unearthly-solemn,*
> *As though you'd been a heaven-supporting column,*
> *Not a dead tree, of bark and foliage stript,*
> *Gigantic eucalypt.*

—Douglas Sladen, 1880

The story of this magnificent Australian tree is very like that of Douglas-fir. These two species, not closely related in any way, have one thing in common: special spiral thickening in the cell walls of their wood give them both an exceptional ability to withstand strain.[173] It was only natural that industrial man would soon realize the value of such timber and eagerly seek it for construction work. Another factor adding to the attack on mountain ash was that its wood is easily split, making it choice material for early house building. Mountain ash, called swamp gum in Tasmania, *Eucalyptus regnans*, was therefore not only avidly logged but was also the victim of raging fires that accompanied this industry and that of land clearing for settlement. The destruction wrought in the early years of the last century was particularly appalling. Today's traveller in Australia or Tasmania will not find the awesomely tall and gigantic trees of the pristine forest, for they are gone. Instead, he will see largely second growth, and it is questionable whether any of this will reach exceptional heights without the protection from wind and drying out that the original forest had.

The mountain ash is one of a huge family of closely related trees, the eucalypts. Within this congenic group are several exceptionally tall species in addition to mountain ash. Indeed, half a dozen have had individual trees of their kind measured very close to or over 91.5 metres (300 feet) high. These are: Alpine ash, *Eucalyptus delegatensis*; karri, *E. diversicolor*; Tasmanian blue gum, *E. globulus*; shining gum, *E. nitens*; messmate stringybark, *E. obliqua*; and manna gum, *E. viminalis*. Currently the tallest non-regnans is a viminalis at 88.8 metres (291.3 feet). The tallest regnans stands at 96.5 metres (316.6 feet) to a dead top. The tallest live foliage is at 92.1 metres (302 feet). Such a close-knit group of tall tree species does not exist elsewhere in the tree world. Of the giant conifers there are only five species, none closely related, that have produced specimens that exceed 300 feet in height, namely: Douglas-fir, *Pseudotsuga menziesii*; coast redwood, *Sequoia sempervirens*; giant sequoia, *Sequoiadendron giganteum*; noble fir, *Abies procera*; and Sitka spruce, *Picea sitchensis*.

It is necessary to go back in time to get a true picture of this singular species of tree, the mountain ash (Figure 23), back to the period of Ferdinand von Mueller, the great botanist who viewed the forest of southeastern Australia when much of it was in its pristine state. Mueller became famous, was knighted and received other honours for his work in Australia. He was intrigued by the stupendous heights of the eucalyptus trees around Melbourne, where he chose to settle. He was too occupied with his plant collections and botanical garden in Melbourne to get out into the ranges to find and measure these very tall trees, so instead he prevailed on others, but his selection was discriminate. He chose surveyors and plant men, people interested in trees, to do this. One in particular was G.W. Robinson of Berwick, a surveyor and civil engineer. Many of the trees that Robinson measured were downed ones, felled by the "timber splitters" for house construction, and he reported that on occasion he was somewhat embarrassed when carrying out his measurements. He once said, "Often when scrambling about over logs and branches to measure a fallen giant, the splitters seemed to regard me with pity, as being a little daft; and when I said a gentleman in Melbourne was anxious to get the measurements, it only increased their pity and they regarded us as both daft."[174]

Robinson began the measurement of trees in the early 1860s in the Dandenong Ranges about 40 kilometres (25 miles) from Melbourne. The paling, shingle or timber splitters were already active there and had been for some time. The tallest tree that

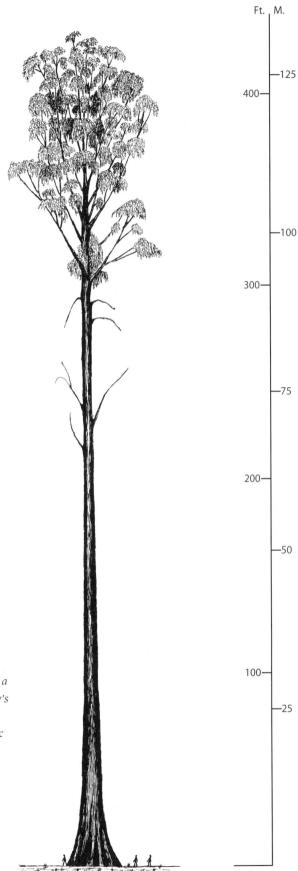

Figure 23: **Mountain ash**,
Eucalyptus regnans

It is necessary to go back in time to get a
true picture of the mountain ash. Today's
traveller in Australia or Tasmania will
not find the awesomely tall and gigantic
mountain ash of the pristine forest, for
they were avidly logged and were the
victim of raging fires that accompanied
land clearing for settlement.

Robinson measured in that area was 104.3 metres (342 feet), but it had some top missing and since the break was 15 centimetres (6 inches) thick he estimated that the full length of the tree could not be less than 109.8 metres (360 feet).[175] Men like Robinson had determined from their measurements that a 2.5-centimetre (1-inch) diameter break represented at least 76 centimetres (2.5 feet) of tree top.

In his report on his tallest measured tree he said that "as the paling-splitters invariably cut down the largest-barrelled trees first in order to get the easiest-splitting timber, I have no doubt but that some of the earlier cut down trees would have measured quite 400 feet [122 metres]". Later, in 1872, Robinson went farther afield into areas largely free of the incursions of the timber splitters, and that year he reported to Mueller that he had measured a tree at the foot of Mount Baw Baw that was 143.6 metres (471 feet) high.[176] Mount Baw Baw is, as the crow flies, about 120 kilometres (75 miles) from Melbourne.

About the time Robinson commenced his measurements for Mueller, David Boyle, a government surveyor from Numawadim near Melbourne, measured a fallen tree in one of the deep recesses of the Dandenongs and found it to be 119.5 metres (392 feet) long. It had a broken-off top, and Boyle added 8.5 metres (28 feet) as a fair estimate, giving a total height of 128 metres (420 feet).[177] He then reported his finding to Mueller.

Robinson and Boyle were just two of the dozen or so enthusiasts who sent in reports to Mueller on the exceptional heights attained by the giant eucalypt of the ranges, the white gum or mountain ash. Mueller reported such findings in scientific journals. Many were undoubtedly conscientiously obtained, but Mueller, it seems, did not personally verify a single one, which means his reports are only second-hand. However, the frequency, the persistence and wide occurrence of the reports indicated that there must be some basis of fact for the statements made.[178]

In time the country around Melbourne and far afield became settled, and great inroads were made into the forested areas. Tracts of forest were felled for timber and for farming, and with this activity came the ravages of fire, which in dry years ran rampant. All this destruction of the forests turned people's attention to the remaining scattered groves, and wonder arose as to what had been before. By 1910 much of the region where the finest stands of mountain ash had prevailed had been cut over, burnt and generally devastated—a truly depressing scene.

In June 1911, old-time surveyor Robinson was asked to present a paper at a meeting in Melbourne of the Field Naturalist Club of Victoria. His theme was a reminiscence of conditions of the past. He said, "It was only after settlement had commenced and roads were opened through the then State forests that bushfires appeared, and began to encroach on the ranges from all sides. The scrub would be burned a little further into the forest each year, so that the present appearance of the ranges is altogether different to what it was sixty years ago. No one who had not seen the districts before these encroachments took place could conceive such an altered appearance, or even believe that perhaps the tallest trees in the world grew there...."[179]

But before this, back in the 1880s, the first stirrings of conscience had arisen that perhaps something should be done to officially record some of these exceptionally tall trees. A prize of £100 was offered to anyone who could point out a tree with a height of 122 metres (400 feet) or more. This prize was never collected though it seems that this was not because such a tree never existed but because very little searching was done to find it. The prize was offered in the winter, with a restricted time limit attached, and only one expedition was made to penetrate a forest not yet assailed by paling splitters, fire or settlement. This lone expedition was not productive as it was inadequately provisioned, and snow, cold and illness compounded the difficulties. Before the three members of the expedition turned back, they did hastily measure one tree and found it to be 99.4 metres (326 feet) high. One of the party, E.J. Dowey, a paling splitter who acted as the expedition's guide, said that when he visited the area later under better weather conditions he saw much taller trees than the one they had measured.[180]

Action to find and measure tall eucalyptus trees continued, but in the early years of the 1900s things were not hopeful and critics arose declaring that no 122-metre (400-foot) trees of E. regnans ever existed. J.H. Maiden, a forester of New South Wales, disclaimed many of the measurements taken in Victoria in the early years. He, in 1907, said that they were simply unreliable. He specifically referred to the detailed measurements of a very tall tree in the Dandenongs made by E.B. Hyne, gardener to Mueller, saying that they could not be depended upon, though he gave no reason for this decision. Dr. A.J. Ewart, a botanist at the Melbourne University, was even more critical. In 1908 he wrote, "The tallest trees in Australia do not appreciably exceed 300 feet [91.5 metres] in height." He pointed to the figures quoted by Mueller, saying that they were all exaggerations and none was based on documentary evidence. He failed to mention, however, certain trees that were measured by surveyors and reported first hand before he gave his paper. There was the Olongolah Tree, 105.8 metres (347 feet) high and measured after felling, named after the parish in which it stood. It was reported on by the engineer of the Shire of Colac. The Baw Baw Tree (sometimes referred to as the New Turkey Tree), 99.4 metres (326 feet) tall, was measured by a team that included a licensed surveyor and a civil engineer. Then there was the tree measured after felling by deputy surveyor Clement Hodgkinson near Coranwordabul Creek, Dandenong Ranges. This had a length of 100.6 metres (330 feet). All these trees were reported first hand, independent of Mueller,[181] and Ewart must have known about them.

The fact is, as already stated, that at the time Maiden and Ewart made their observations on the height of eucalyptus trees, particularly E. regnans, the extensive forests of Victoria were in a sad and degraded condition, riddled by the activities of the timber merchants, settlers and fire. Despite this onslaught, a few tall trees were come upon subsequently. For example, there was the Gerraty Tree, which was blown down in 1939. It would probably never have been measured if its log had not lain across a forest road, blocking the way of a party of foresters that included F.G. Gerraty, inspector of forests, in company with the chairman of the Forest Commission who was visiting the area at the time. The log had to be sawn through to permit passage, and while this was being done, Gerraty measured the length of the tree that had such a superb log. It turned out to be 106.1 metres (348 feet).[182] Some ten years later a very tall tree in the

Toorongo forest was measured after felling. Its length was 101.2 metres (332 feet) to a broken top, where the diameter was 15 centimetres (6 inches). The estimated total height was 104 metres (341 feet).[183]

For many years the maximum height attained by *E. regnans* seemed to be officially taken as 114.3 metres (375 feet)—that of the Cornthwaite Tree, also known as the Thorpdale Tree after the district in which it stood. George Cornthwaite, certified surveyor, measured the tree by instrument in 1880. Next year it was felled for lumber. He then measured it by tape and there was close agreement.[184] Here the matter rested. All reports of taller trees were disregarded because they lacked firm documentation, although there were scattered references in the literature to Robinson's 143.6-metre (471-foot) tree, which he came upon and measured near the foot of Mount Baw Baw in 1872.[185] But Robinson, as was his wont, reported his finding to Mueller and the tree was thus presumably regarded as reported second hand.

In the early 1980s Ken Simpfendorfer, special projects officer in the Department of Conservation, Forests and Lands, Melbourne, initiated research into all accounts, new and old, of big trees in Victoria. It was under his direction that William Ferguson's report of a 132.3-metre (434-foot) tree, measured by him in 1872, came to light. Ferguson was Inspector of State Forests at the time and was under instructions from the assistant commissioner of Lands and Survey, Clement Hodgkinson.

According to Simpfendorfer, Ferguson's report appeared authentic, but it was directed to departmental files and did not appear in any later references. It thus disappeared from public knowledge.[186] Even Mueller made no reference to it, and this is understandable because there was a deal of hate between Mueller and Ferguson. It was Ferguson who, a few years prior, had contested Mueller and had had him driven from the botanical garden in Melbourne, which Mueller had founded and carefully tended for many years.[187] Ferguson's finding, however, did not pass entirely unannounced, as one William Macready mentioned it in a letter to the *Argus*, a contemporary Melbourne newspaper.[188]

The Ferguson Tree was a downed tree, burnt by fire at the base and toppled by wind. Its trunk diameter 1.5 metres (5 feet) from the ground was 5.5 metres (18 feet) and its colossal log spanned a deep ravine. A large part of its top was missing and the break, at 132.3 metres (434 feet) from its base, had a diameter of 91 centimetres (3 feet), indicating that it must have been all of 152.4 metres (500 feet) high originally. Ferguson was surveying stands of timber in the Watts River area tributary to the Yarra, and at that time the forests there had not been penetrated by the timber splitters.[189] Ferguson's report gives strong validation to the reports of others made in the early years to Mueller.

It must be remembered that the measurements given in some of Mueller's reports of exceptionally tall trees were initially obtained by certified surveyors. This, of course, does not entirely preclude exaggeration or error but it does make them less likely. Such is the case with the tree measured by John Rollo of Yarragan with a height of 125 metres (410 feet), and the same may be said for the tree near Mount Sabine measured by Colonel Ellery in company with Prof. Wilson, who found the trunk 6.6 metres (21.7

feet) thick where cut, with a length, including the stump, of 115.9 metres (380 feet). In the same category is the tree already described, measured by David Boyle, with a length of 128 metres (420 feet).[190]

A unique feature that many species of eucalypts share is the great length of bole clear of branches. The Cornthwaite Tree had a "clear barrel" to 76.2 metres (250 feet). This was an admirable height, but not exceptional for an *E. regnans*. E.B. Heyne, Mueller's gardener, measured a fallen mountain ash in the Dandenongs that had a clear trunk for 89.9 metres (295 feet) and government surveyor Boyle reported finding a tree of this species that was branchless for 92.1 metres (302 feet).[191] N.J. Caire, a noted tree photographer, reported a tree at Childers, South Gippsland, that was 91.5 metres (300 feet) to where the branches began and from there reached upward another 15.2 metres (50 feet).[192]

Although a giant in height and width of bole at ground line, mountain ash trees produce no record volumes of timber. This is because of the trunk's rapid taper immediately after it leaves the ground. Few trees now standing have trunks over 4.3 metres (14 feet) thick at breast height, but things were different when the white man first came upon the scene. Descriptions and photographs of many of these giants are on record. Robinson and Boyle report measuring trees 7.9 metres (25.8 feet) in diameter at 1.22 metres (4 feet) above the ground. Mueller received reports from Hobart, Tasmania, of a living tree near Mount Wellington with a bole 9.9 metres (32.5 feet) thick at 90 centimetres (3 feet) above the ground. The base diameter was 12.6 metres (41.4 feet). There is the Bulga Stump near Bulga, South Gippsland. Photographs of it were taken before it was consumed by flames about 1890. Before that it had a breast-height diameter of 10.8 metres (35.5 feet) as calculated from its circumference.[193]

Many of these huge eucalypts were hollow. One with an inside diameter of 7.9 metres (26 feet) was used as a church and school, and later as a stable for five horses. It succumbed to fire in 1898. In 1890 a photograph was taken of a family living in a hollow tree near Neerin. Two children shown were born there.

All evidence indicates that most species of eucalyptus trees are not long lived. The maximum age of mountain ash appears to be about 450 years. Few stands of it have lasted many hundreds of years before being destroyed by fire. One of the oldest, largest and healthiest trees known was the giant on Nicholls Spur near Junee, Tasmania. It was 394 years old when felled in 1942. All indications were that it would have lived for another century.[194]

Karri

Eucalyptus diversicolor

Australia is the realm of the eucalypt. This race of trees is widespread over the continent and probably has been since Australia drifted away from the vast southern landmass of Gondwanaland 15 to 60 million years ago. As it moved north it came under warmer and drier conditions, and deserts and treeless plains appeared over much of the continent, but the southwest corner still extended far enough south to come under the influence of the moist westerly winds. Therefore some moisture fell there even in the drier summer season, and instead of desert or semi-arid country, lush vegetation continued to flourish, although the area was not at all extensive. This condition of things intensified as the glaciers of the last ice age retreated.

During many millennia following the ice age, plant life in this corner of the continent carried on in comparative isolation, and a degree of divergence from the flora of the rest of the continent developed. Some exceptional trees arose. One, karri, *Eucalyptus diversicolor*, took advantage of its tendency to height and developed into one of the most majestic trees on earth (Figure 24). It is unfortunate that there are so few of them, but its area of incidence is small, being some 145 kilometres (90 miles) long by 40 kilometres (25 miles) wide plus a few restricted outliers.

The word "karri" is an aboriginal name. The specific part of the botanical name, *"diversicolor,"* refers to the many shades of its smooth bark, which on the whole is a very light grey or near white. Karri, despite its giant size and height, is a graceful, queenly tree with an ashlike bole clear of branches to a great height. Sadly, many of the finest trees are gone, felled for timber. The tallest now standing is Stewart's Karri near the Donnelly River about 16 kilometres (10 miles) west of the town of Manjimup. It is 84 metres (275.6 feet) high with a clear bole of 48.5 metres (159 feet) that is 2.3 metres (7.7 feet) thick at a man's breast height.[195]

Taller trees have been accurately measured in former times. In 1921 a downed tree was come upon by a party of surveyors between the Gardner and Shannon rivers about 13 kilometres (8 miles) east of Northcliffe. This is about the centre of the main karri country. It was 100.6 metres (330 feet) long.[196] Earlier, in 1916, standing trees were measured near Pemberton (then Big Brook) that were 91.5 metres (300 feet) high. Some of these had a "clear barrel" to 54.9 metres (180 feet) and one to 61 metres (200 feet).[197]

For such a tall tree the trunk of a karri is slim. The most reliable measurement of a maximum size of bole is 4.6 metres (15 feet) in diameter at breast height and 5.2 metres (17 feet) at ground level. This measurement was made in 1916 on a tree southwest of Pemberton that has since disappeared.[198] A hollow tree standing in the town park at

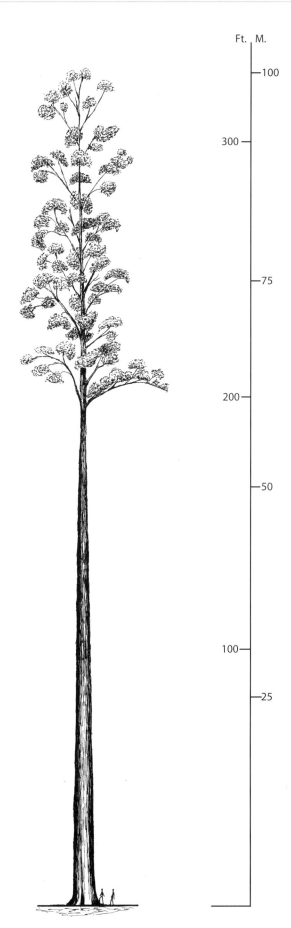

Figure 24: **Karri**,
Eucalyptus diversicolor

Karri, despite its giant size and height, is a graceful, queenly eucalypt with an ashlike bole clear of branches to a great height. The tallest now standing is Stewart's Karri, at 84 metres (275.6 feet) high.

Northcliffe is 4.3 metres (14 feet) wide. The Hawke Tree, also still standing, about 16 kilometres (10 miles) southwest of Pemberton, has a trunk diameter at breast height of 3.6 metres (11.9 feet).[199]

Like most eucalypt species, karri does not live to a great age. It is generally considered that 500 years is about the limit. The Underwood Tree, an ancient giant in Beedelup Park, about 16 kilometres (10 miles) west of Pemberton, is thought to be at least 400 years old.[200]

A forest of karri with its high canopy supported by slender white pillars emerging from the green undergrowth shrubbery is a wondrous sight, well worth travelling many thousands of miles to see.

Messmate stringybark

Eucalyptus obliqua

This is a towering timber tree that has been much logged in southeastern Australia and Tasmania, with its most majestic stands in the latter territory. It is usually referred to as the third tallest Australian tree species after the giant mountain ash, *Eucalyptus regnans*, and the karri, *E. diversicolor*, that imposing tree of southwestern Australia. The extreme height of currently existing messmate stringybark is 78 metres (256 feet), and the greatest breast-height trunk diameter of a tree now standing is 5.2 metres (17.2 feet), a specimen in the Styx Valley area of Tasmania.[201] In the middle of the last century, qualified surveyors documented taller trees that measured up to 98.8 metres (324 feet), but those in the forest of the Florentine Valley of south-central Tasmania now show senescence and have lost height, possibly due to logging activities that have opened up the forest, thereby increasing desiccation and wind injury. Older documents tell of even larger specimens. A government report of 1914 states that the species reached a height of 106.7 metres (350 feet) and could be branchless to 76.2 metres (250 feet) from the ground, and that there were trees with a bole diameter of 6.4 metres (21 feet).[202] The great width of trunk is often carried up to where the branches begin, which can be 61 metres (200 feet) (Figure 25). Messmate stringybark is a notable tree but not quite in the category of mountain ash.

It is tempting to question the veracity of these old records, such as those given above for *E. obliqua*. There is certainly no standing blue gum tree, *E. globulus*, near 91.5 metres (300 feet) high. However, there were trees in southeastern Tasmania that

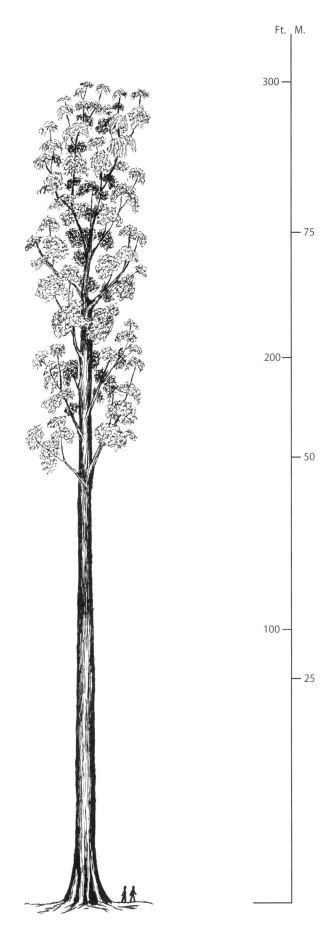

Ft. M.

300

75

200

50

100

25

Figure 25: **Messmate stringybark**,
Eucalyptus obliqua

*The messmate stringybark is the third
tallest Australian tree. Specimens have
been recorded up to 106.7 metres (350
feet) in height. The extreme height of
currently existing messmate stringybark
in the Styx Valley area of Tasmania is 78
metres (256 feet).*

exceeded this height at the time the first Europeans settled there, and two tall trees stood into quite recent times south of Hobart, one 94.5 metres (310 feet) and another 97 metres (318 feet) high. One of them had a "clean barrel" for 63.4 metres (208 feet).[203] Both were well known and fully documented, and the same may well apply to *E. obliqua*.

While on the subject of the great heights of eucalyptus trees, it is well to mention that there are other species of this race that reach up to great heights. Exceptional specimens of manna gum, *E. viminalis*, alpine ash, *E. delegatensis*, and shining gum, *E. nitens*, have been measured that almost touch the 91.5-metre (300-foot) mark.[204] All these species inhabit suitably moist areas of southeastern Australia or Tasmania.

Alerce or Patagonian cypress

Fitzroya cupressoides

Far away in southern Chile and Patagonia there is a relic of the past rather along the lines of the coast and Sierra redwoods of California. Alerce (pronounced ah-lair-say) as it is popularly called is also known as Patagonian cypress. Because of the excellence of its timber it has been heavily exploited for several centuries, starting in the mid-1500s, so that now all the best lowland stands have disappeared.

Some of the old records of alerce are scarcely credible: that 4,000 annual growth rings were counted on the trunks of some trees; that others were 12.2 metres (40 feet) in basal diameter and still others 73.2 metres (240 feet) in length. Current measurements of trees now standing are less, but since we are dealing with what the species is capable of in the absolute, historical records must be taken into account. Close examination of the sources of the early records indicates that many have a strong element of truth. Thus the maximum size records would appear to be 70.1 metres (230 feet) for height, 4.6 metres (15 feet) for diameter of bole at the height of a man's breast (Figure 26) and an extreme age of 3,622 years.[205]

Trees open-grown in arboreta and gardens retain their branches down to the ground, but this is not the way they grow in the forest. The trunk of old-growth trees, straight and cylindrical, may be clear of branches so that only the upper portion of the tree is richly clothed with verdure. The bark of a mature tree is about 5 centimetres (2 inches) thick, red brown and furrowed and will peel off in long strips. The leaves are dark green, tiny, pointed, about 3 millimetres (0.12 inches) long and are arranged

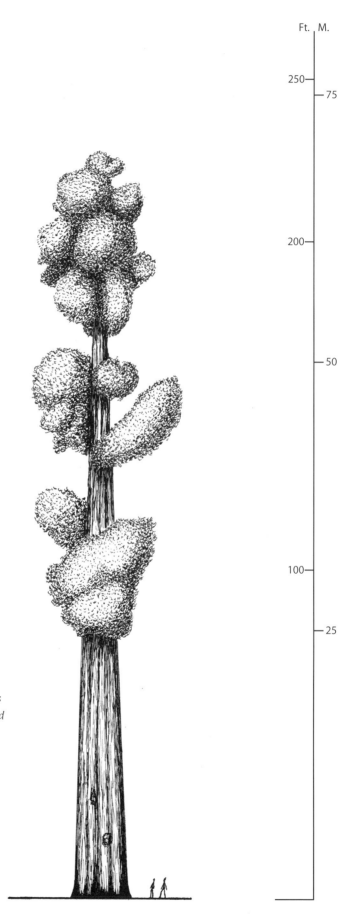

Figure 26: **Alerce** *or* **Patagonian cypress**, Fitzroya cupressoides

Alerce thrives under wet, cool conditions where the release of nutrients is slow and sparse. Growth is extremely slow and it is only because of the ability to live such an enormous span of time that it becomes a giant tree.

in alternate whorls of three. The cones are small, not more than 6 millimetres (0.25 inches) across.

Alerce can form dense, almost pure stands. Before the inroads of logging it grew down to sea level but now is mostly found at elevations of 610 to 915 metres (2,000 to 3,000 feet). Its growth is so slow as to be almost imperceptible on a yearly basis. It is only because of its ability to live such an enormous span of time that it becomes a giant tree. It thrives under wet, cool conditions where the release of nutrients is slow and sparse. Annual precipitation exceeds 2,540 millimetres (100 inches) in most areas where it grows.

Here is a species that appears natively in one small tract of planet Earth. The majority of the stands are in Chile, with the remainder in Argentina. Its prime habitat is from Valdivia south beyond Puerto Montt, including the Island of Chiloe where it was viewed by Captain Fitzroy and Charles Darwin when on Darwin's epic voyage of 1831–36. It was from Fitzroy that the tree obtained the generic part of its botanical name. Exploitation of its much valued timber was already underway, but members of Fitzroy's ship did take measurements. Alerce has been ruthlessly logged and cut over. Its timber, besides being easily worked, beautifully veined and coloured a rich reddish brown, is extraordinarily durable, being highly resistant to fungal and insect attack. It is claimed that logs lying on the ground for two centuries remain sound.

TROPICS

Silk-cotton tree

Ceiba pentandra

Different varieties of this tree can be found in most tropical countries, but what is dealt with here is but one variety—the giant form, var. *caribaea*—and it can grow to a prodigious size. It seems that it arose in the jungles of Central America or Amazonia. Then at some pre-Colombian time its fruit or seed was transported via sea currents to the west coast of Africa. From there it spread into the interior of this continent and can now be found as far south as Angola, and east to Malawi and the Great Rift Valley of Tanzania and Kenya. It was aided in this by its wind-borne seed and by humans, who found its rapid growth and wide-spread canopy made it a good shade tree and planted it near settlements.

The silk-cotton tree has several characteristics superbly evolved to ensure its survival and dispersal amid the fierce competition of the tropical rain forest. Foremost perhaps is its size. It can grow tall and thrust out head and shoulders above the general rain forest canopy—it is a true emergent tree. Its giant size can support a wide-spreading crown and in this way expose a vast array of foliage to the all-important sun. The dispersal question is nicely addressed too. Seeds travel a good distance because the branches are so high, but more important is the fibre of floss attached to each of its seeds, which ensures that the seed is carried away by the wind. Since the fibre is hollow, the seed will also float on the waters of the rivers or the sea. Moreover, humans found the floss useful and introduced yet another means of transport of the seed—the floss was used as cushioning and was traded around without removing the seed. It is this silky fluff that has given the tree its other name of kapok.

In the Americas it is an enormous tree and its vast domes of foliage, towering above the general level of the jungle canopy, are a conspicuous sight viewed from the rivers.[206] These huge umbrellalike domes can be as much as 45 metres (150 feet) wide. Trees have been found that have boles 2.4 metres (8 feet) thick above the buttresses and at a man's breast height are as much as 8.2 metres (27 feet) in diameter including the buttresses.[207] The top of the dome is occasionally 49 metres (160 feet) high.

So outstanding was the silk-cotton tree in the Americas that it was singled out by the ancient Maya people, and they looked upon it with awe. It was called the Yax-cheel-cab or "The First Tree of the World" and is part of Mayan mythology. Anthropologists believe that this legend may have arisen from one magnificent specimen.[208]

The general configuration of the tree is the same in Africa, but the trunk is extended before the out-throw of branches so the tree is taller. Trees there have been known to reach a height of 70 metres (230 feet) or more.[209] The crest of the great dome of the famous tree at Freetown, Sierra Leone, is 75 metres (246 feet) high, and the canopy span is 50 metres (164 feet). Its trunk above the buttresses is 2.4 metres (7.8 feet) thick and at breast height including the buttresses is 4.8 metres (15.7 feet). The great branches forming the canopy jut out over 30 metres (100 feet) from the ground.[210] Doubtless the silk-cotton tree is the tallest of all the continent's trees. The fact that they reach these heights in Africa while the tops of the vast domes of the American trees

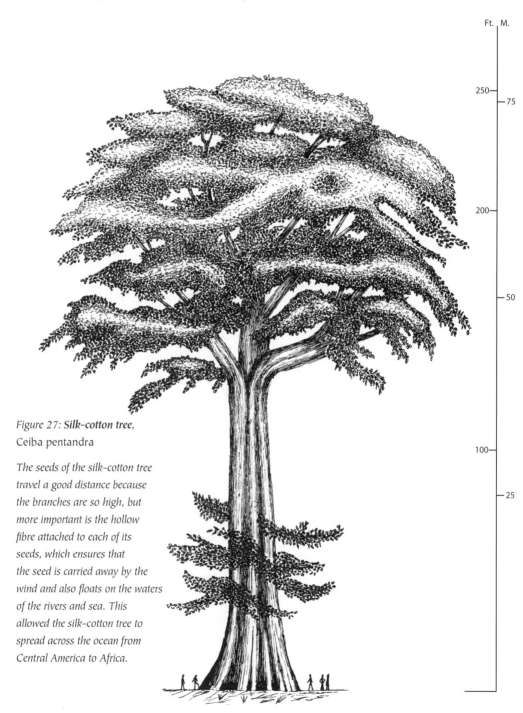

Figure 27: **Silk-cotton tree**,
Ceiba pentandra

The seeds of the silk-cotton tree travel a good distance because the branches are so high, but more important is the hollow fibre attached to each of its seeds, which ensures that the seed is carried away by the wind and also floats on the waters of the rivers and sea. This allowed the silk-cotton tree to spread across the ocean from Central America to Africa.

Ft.   M.

250—
    —75

200—

    —50

100—

    —25

hardly attain 61 metres (200 feet) is possibly due to the generally higher canopy level of African trees. In the high forest of Liberia, silk-cotton trees have been measured whose boles rise 36.6 metres (120 feet) free of branches.[211]

The bole of the silk-cotton tree is straight and massive but not always cylindrical. The buttresses are often planklike, 15 to 30 centimetres (6 to 12 inches) thick and may extend up the bole 6 metres (20 feet) or more. They sometimes divide widely at the base, forming cubicles. Where they leave the trunk, the main branches are also buttressed by triangular brackets at the upper side (note sketch at right). The bark of older trees is ashy grey; young trees may have thorns. The wood is poor and of little use. The leaves are of fair size, digitately compound, made up of five to eight leaflets each about 15 centimetres (6 inches) long. The flowers are white, have a fetid odor and are pollinated by bats. The fruit is a leathery capsule that splits into several segments when ripe, releasing the seed.

Figure 27 depicts the awesome proportions of the tree at Freetown—its great height, expansive crown and stupendous structure. It is thought to be about 250 years old. It was under the shade of this tree that many slaves were freed some 200 years ago.

Baobab

Adansonia digitata

Figure 28 presents a tree that is quite grotesque, the baobab, and the specimen shown is rather more handsome than many of its kind. Every stem of the baobab is swollen and stubby. This is to accommodate the storage of water, as this tree is an inhabitant of the semi-arid regions of Africa. In order to store water it develops an enormous bole, which in some cases rivals the largest in the world. On average this may be 4.6 to 6.1 metres (15 to 20 feet) thick, but large specimens can have a diameter much greater. The bole of the tree at Sagole, Northern Transvaal, is 10.8 metres (35.4 feet) thick.

There is another huge tree 160 kilometres (100 miles) south at Duiwelskloof, also in the Transvaal, that is just as big as this, but this tree may in fact be two trees growing very close together that have become fused.[212]

The obesity of the trunk not only depends on the age of the tree but also on the amount of water it contains, as it swells during rainy periods and shrinks in times of drought. The leaves of the baobab are palmately compound, moderate in size. The flowers are white and showy.

Although the trunk is enormous, the tree is not tall, the tallest recorded being 30.5 metres (100 feet). This tree was situated near Victoria Falls on the Zambezi River.

Ft.   M.

100—

—25

*Figure 28: **Baobab**, Adansonia digitata*

The stem of the baobab is swollen and stubby in order to accommodate storage of water in the semi-arid regions of Africa. The enormous bole not only depends on the age of the tree but also on the amount of water it contains, swelling during rainy periods and shrinking in times of drought.

Because of the expansive trunk, the crown span can be considerable, up to 45.7 metres (150 feet). The spread of the roots in their search for water can be much greater, in some cases reaching out for 90 metres (300 feet) from the base of the trunk, giving a total span of over 180 metres (600 feet). The bark is a metallic grey and on old trees can be 15 centimetres (6 inches) or more thick. The wood is worthless as timber, as its function is largely to absorb and store water. However, many parts of the baobab are much used by the indigenous people. The bark is used for roofing and the bark fibres for rope and floor mats. The seeds and leaves are eaten and the pulp enclosing the seeds is made into a drink. Small bulbs at the roots' ends are dug up, dried and ground to make porridge.

There are baobabs whose width of trunk is greater than the height of the tree. It is so singular in appearance that many expressions have been used to describe it: bizarre, weird, monstrous, fantastic—all very fitting terms. It has been referred to by the aboriginal people as the upside-down tree, an especially apt name in the dry season when the tree is leafless and the stubby branches assume the appearance of roots.

Baobabs can live a long time. Some of the larger trees are thought to be 3,000 and even 4,000 years old.[213] Radio-carbon dating of a tree with a moderate-sized 4.5-metre (14.8-foot) diameter trunk gave an age of 1,000 years. Apparently the early explorers who came upon these huge trees were overly impressed by the size of the trunk, proclaiming ages of 5,000 to 6,000 years. The vitality of the baobab is remarkable.

Even after its interior is completely destroyed it will continue to flourish, and the shell may be used as a house, stable or storage shed.[214]

The baobab may be described as the most accommodating of trees. It begins life without fuss, grows enormous slowly and after some 3,000 or more years it breaks down within itself. The whole then crumbles into a mass of fibrous pulp that in time is consumed by spontaneous burning, so in the end all is cleaned up, leaving no mess at all.[215]

A mystery of the baobab is that in the whole of Africa, where the tree is widespread, there is only one species, whereas in Madagascar, an island of limited size, there are seven distinct species. Two of the Madagascar species are more majestic than the African one because of the increased height of their bloated trunks, which may extend for 25 metres (80 feet) or more, topped by absurdly small crowns of foliage. The trunk tapers very little right up to where the stubby branches jut out, but is smaller in diameter than that of the African tree.

There is a single species in the northwest territory of Australia. It tends to be more squat than its African cousin but is otherwise similar. Vincent Serventy, the outstanding Australian naturalist and author, postulated that at some time, perhaps several millennia ago, seed of the African tree was carried by ocean currents to the Australian shore.[216]

Dahoma

Piptodeniastrum africanum

Dahoma is a gigantic tree with a lofty, wide-spreading crown. To find a place in the sun, dahoma does not grow extremely tall but throws out branches at an incline that reach far up. Its configuration is therefore rather individualistic. The tree seems quite successful as its distribution is widespread in Africa, where it can be found in Senegal, Nigeria, Congo, south to Angola and east as far as Malawi. In all these countries there are flourishing forests with which it must contend.

Dahoma's vast canopy possibly makes it appear more immense than it otherwise would. Its bole, although impressive, tall and cylindrical, supported by prominent buttresses, is not as large as those of some giant African trees. The buttresses extend up 6 metres (20 feet) or more and the bole here may be 1.8 metres (6 feet) thick and rise another 9 to 15 metres (30 to 50 feet) before branching out. Total maximum height is 51.8 metres (170 feet), usually just enough to permit it to tower above the average canopy[217] (note Figure 29). Dahoma cannot be said to be in the same class as some emergent African trees that reach heights of over 61 metres (200 feet).

Figure 29: **Dahoma**, Piptodeniastrum africanum

The dahoma is a lacy, even delicate, tree. The upper branchlets are slender and the frondlike foliage is small and fine, permitting strong winds to pass through freely. The bark of the bole and branches is smooth and a pure grey, adding to the tree's attractiveness.

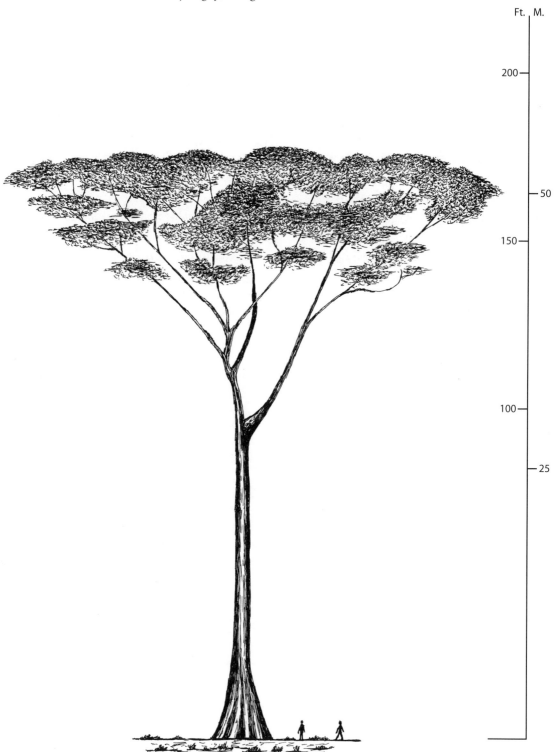

Dahoma, sometimes called dabema, has developed special features to support its umbrellalike crown. The buttresses are exceedingly well developed and in fact are about the ultimate for this form of support. They are planklike, extend well up the bole, and at the tree's base radiate out over the ground for more than 6 metres (20 feet), curving and dividing, their ribs rising 15 to 30 centimetres (6 to 12 inches) above the ground. Even the major branches, as they leave the trunk, have flanges on their upper sides for added support since they splay out sideways rather widely to support the expansive canopy. The wood has interlocking fibres that give strength to the bole and branches, an advantage in time of storm.[218]

It is of interest to note what various species of trees do to ensure a place in the sun. The adaptations acquired by dahoma are indeed unique. A tree in New Zealand, the kauri, *Agathis australis*, has a spreading, branching habit too, along with suitable height to accomplish the same positioning of its foliage. However, it does not rely on flanges to support its expansive crown but on bulk plus sturdiness, and this means it has an enormous bole. Also the kauri has no buttresses but relies on extraordinary root structures. Deep in the soil it develops large plate-like knobs that are attached to certain major roots and are designed to anchor it in time of storm.[219]

Despite its immense proportions, dahoma is in some ways a lacy, even delicate, tree. The upper branchlets are slender and the foliage is small and fine, permitting strong winds to pass through freely. It is a mimosa, a legume with doubly compound, frondlike leaves about 15 centimetres (6 inches) long with tiny leaflets. The bark of the bole and branches is smooth and a pure grey, adding to the tree's attractiveness.

Tapang

Koompassia excelsa

This is the tallest of all broadleaf tropical rainforest trees. It is a true jungle tree, found throughout the lowland forest of the East Indies except in peat swamps. It has different common names depending on the country in which it is growing. In Sarawak it is called tapang; in peninsular Malaysia, tualang; and in Sabah, mengaris. Since it is rather common in Sarawak and the tallest trees are there, the name "tapang" is used here. Botanically it is known as *Koompassia excelsa*. It is a legume, whereas most trees of the tropical forests of the East Indies are of other races.

A tapang in peninsular Malaysia measured out at 80.8 metres (265 feet) high, while trees of this species in Sarawak were found that reached 83.8 and 86 metres (275 and 282 feet).[220] These are remarkable heights for jungle trees, especially since there is nothing like them in the expansive tropical forest of Africa or South America. However, many of the tree species where tapang grows are huge and tall. A race of trees known as the dipterocarps makes up a large proportion of the forest there, and it comprises many giant species. There are other associations of giant trees, too, so if a species aspires to be an emergent in this region it must be exceptionally lofty. A list of the tall tree species with which tapang must contend is interesting:

Botanical name	Maximum height	Species' family name
Shorea curtisii	68.6 metres (225 feet)	Dipterocarpaceae
S. pauciflora	68.6 metres (225 feet)	Dipterocarpaceae
S. superba	75 metres (246 feet)	Dipterocarpaceae
Dryobalanops aromatica	76.2 metres (250 feet)	Dipterocarpaceae
Anisoptera costata	64 metres (210 feet)	Dipterocarpaceae
Neobalanocarpus heimii	61 metres (200 feet)	Dipterocarpaceae
Dyera costulata	76.2 metres (250 feet)	Apocynaceae
Eucalyptus deglupta	78 metres (256 feet)	Myrtaceae

Foresters have reported that in places in the forests of Malaysia the average level of the tree canopy can be as much as 61 metres (200 feet). This is an exceptional height for a tropical rainforest canopy.

The bole of a giant tapang tree is a wondrous sight. The huge buttresses may extend up the bole for 9 metres (30 feet), where they taper off to a tremendous trunk 3 metres (10 feet) thick. This structure can rise unbranched for another 36.6 metres (120 feet).[221] It is cylindrical, hard and smooth, and often coloured a pale fluorescent green. The crown is oval in outline and wide-spread (Figure 30). Since the tree is a legume, the leaves are pinnate and rather dainty. The seed is surrounded by a papery wing, which aids in its distribution.

When the forest is cleared for farming or felled for timber, tapang trees are often left standing. There are several reasons for this. They are good honey trees, and the local people market the honey and the wax from the combs so do not wish them destroyed. Also, they view the tapang tree with awe, believing it to be associated with spirits, or even to be haunted. This may be due to the tree's ability to heal itself rapidly when a large branch breaks away. The huge buttresses and size of the trees make them difficult to fell and handle so the wood cutters tend to leave them alone. Moreover, the wood is hard, heavy and not easily worked.

The bees select tapang trees as they offer protection from sun bears, their chief predator other than humans. The smooth hard bark and wood of the tapang make it difficult for the bears to claw their way up, but man is more resourceful and uses bamboo climbing pegs driven into the tree's bole to climb to the bees' nests, which are attached high up on the branches, suspended in teardrop fashion.

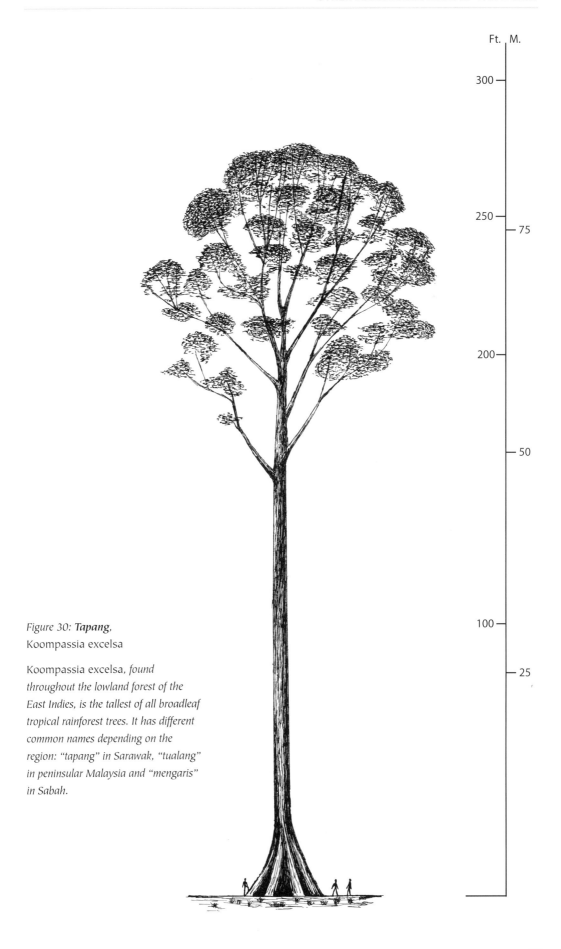

Figure 30: **Tapang**,
Koompassia excelsa

Koompassia excelsa, *found
throughout the lowland forest of the
East Indies, is the tallest of all broadleaf
tropical rainforest trees. It has different
common names depending on the
region: "tapang" in Sarawak, "tualang"
in peninsular Malaysia and "mengaris"
in Sabah.*

Kapur

Dryobalanops aromatica

In the forests of Indo-Malaysia there is a race of giant trees called dipterocarps because of the two wings appended to the seed of the tree (see p. 92). This family consists of several hundred species. Many are huge and lofty trees. Most mature dipterocarps reach a height of 61 metres (200 feet) but some, such as kapur, *Dryobalanops aromatica*, decidedly exceed this and are true emergents (Figure 31). However, not all emergent trees in the lowland forest of Indo-Malaysia are dipterocarps. There are trees of other races also such as *Dyera costulata* (Apocynaceae family), *Agathis dammara* (Araucariaceae) and *Eucalyptus deglupta* (Myrtaceae). Then, of course, there is the tallest giant broadleaf tree of all, which has already been dealt with, *Koompassia excelsa* of the Leguminaceae family.

Kapur is a giant tree in all respects. Its bole is spectacular, huge, straight, cylindrical and sometimes rising 46 metres (150 feet) above the forest floor before branching out. Total height can be as much as 76.2 metres (250 feet). The support buttresses are massive and may extend up the trunk for 6 metres (20 feet) before tapering off to a bole 3.7 metres (12 feet) thick. The crown is wide-spread.[222] The trunk is a purple brown and the bark is coarsely fissured. This aids vinelike plants such as lianas to reach into the canopy. Lianas can be huge, sometimes as thick in stem as a man's thigh and more than 100 metres (328 feet) long. They rely on free-standing trees for support. Some cling to the tree's bole, while others hang loosely and attach themselves by various means to the tree's upper branches, from which they hang in loops and festoons.

Kapur, or camphorwood as it is known in Borneo, is a lowland evergreen tree but not of the peat swamp lands. The leaves, as with all dipterocarps, are simple with smooth margins, broadly ovate, and about 10 centimetres (4 inches) long. The flowers are not overly showy and are pollinated by insects. It is an important timber tree.

The forests where kapur grows are taller than any other broadleaf tropical rain forest in the world. In certain localities the average canopy height is 61 metres (200 feet). In the expansive tropical forest of the Amazon and the Americas as a whole, even the emergent trees rarely attain or surpass this height. Some of the giant trees of Africa are somewhat loftier, but they are rare. Yet kapur can loom up above the highest level of the Indo-Malayan forest canopy by 15 metres (50 feet)![223]

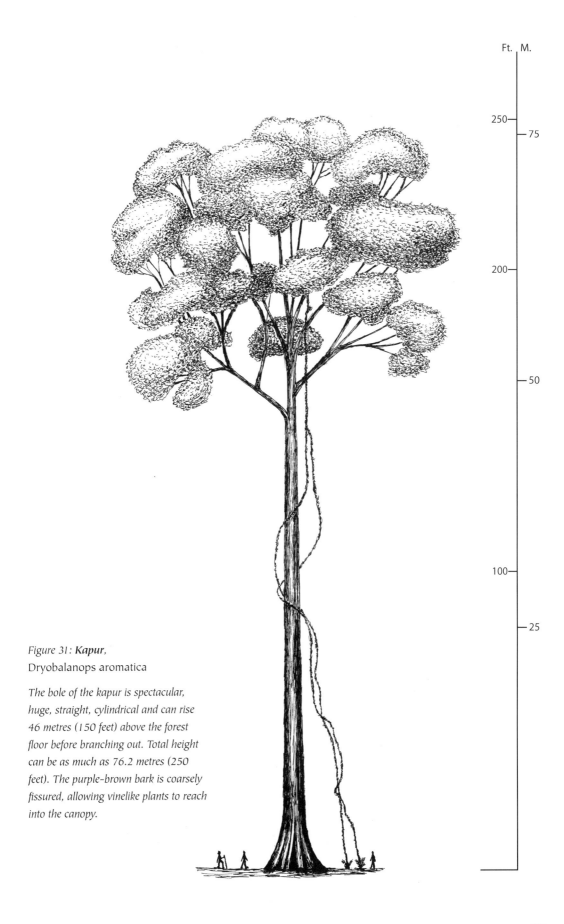

Ft. M.

250 — 75

200 — 50

100 — 25

Figure 31: **Kapur**,
Dryobalanops aromatica

*The bole of the kapur is spectacular,
huge, straight, cylindrical and can rise
46 metres (150 feet) above the forest
floor before branching out. Total height
can be as much as 76.2 metres (250
feet). The purple-brown bark is coarsely
fissured, allowing vinelike plants to reach
into the canopy.*

Klinki pine

Araucaria hunsteinii

Here is a species of tree whose ancestors established themselves in Gondwanaland, the huge continent that 100 million years ago centred around the south pole and of which Antarctica is the remnant. Australia split away and started its northward drift about 45 million years ago, taking the fledgling klinki pine with it, plus a number of its kind, the Araucariaceae. Certain of these now inhabit Australia, New Zealand, southern South America, New Guinea and some islands of the South Pacific. Two of the closest related and most similar in appearance to klinki pine are hoop pine (*Araucaria cunninghamii*) and bunya pine (*A. bidwillii*), both of Australia. These are stately and lofty trees but not as tall as the klinki pine of Papua New Guinea.

Klinki pine is quite exceptional, quite unlike its companion broadleaf trees in the tropical rain forest in form and shape. It is sometimes seen towering 30 metres (100 feet) above the general jungle canopy.[224] It bears a prehistoric appearance, which is not surprising as it is a survivor from long ago. The bole is carried undivided to the top of the crown. The branches jut out from the trunk more or less horizontally in regular tiers, and the foliage is held in tufts at the branch ends (Figure 32).

Klinki pine breaks all height records for tropical rainforest trees. As has been pointed out, a giant broadleaf tree, a tapang in Sarawak, Borneo, was found that scaled 86 metres (282 feet) high, but a klinki pine showed a measurement of 89 metres (292 feet)—the tallest tropical tree ever recorded.[225] The trunk can be majestic, sometimes nearly 3 metres (10 feet) thick and branch free for 30 metres (100 feet) up.[226] The oldest tree so far found attained 700 years.

The bark of mature trees of klinki pine is hard, rough and very dark brownish grey. The foliage consists of two ranked rows of close, stiff, flattish needles some 5 centimetres (2 inches) long. It is not at all attractive to browsing animals, and this fact may have been of value to the tree in ancestral times. The cones are globular and about 5 centimetres (2 inches) wide. The seeds are of good size and much sought by birds.

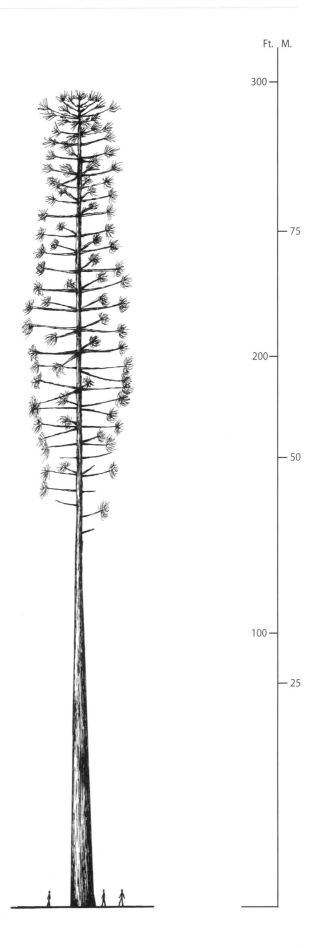

*Figure 32: **Klinki pine**,*
Araucaria hunsteinii

*Klinki pine is exceptional in form and
shape. The bole is carried undivided
to the top of the crown. The branches
jut out from the trunk more or less
horizontally in regular tiers, and the
foliage is held in tufts at the branch
ends. Bark is hard, rough and a very
dark brownish grey. This prehistoric
appearance is not surprising as the klinki
is a survivor from long ago.*

Brazil-nut tree

Bertholletia excelsa

This is an emergent tree of the Amazon jungle, not only mighty in stature but also beautifully formed. Its trunk is straight without swellings or supporting buttresses and can rise branch free for 30 to 40 metres (100 to 130 feet). The topmost boughs can be 60 metres (200 feet) from the ground. The trunk at a man's breast height can be over 4 metres (13 feet) thick.[227] Its bark is furrowed and a rich brown. The grandeur of the tree is enhanced by a high, broad canopy of large, flat, elliptical leaves. It can live for 1,000 years (Figure 33).

The flowers of the Brazil-nut tree are pale yellow and held in panicles. On fertilization the flowers develop into spherical woody fruits up to 15 centimetres (6 inches) in diameter and 1.4 kilograms (3 pounds) in weight. Inside the capsule are 12 to 24 hard-shelled nuts, the seed of the fruit, which are closely packed like the segments of an orange.[228] This cannon-ball-like fruit can kill when it drops from a great height and strikes an unprotected person. The rock-hard carapace of the fruit does not break when it hits the ground. Distribution and continuance of the species is dependent on a large rodent, the agouti, which chews through the outer shell and those of the nuts within. This animal stores some of the nuts in caches, sometimes quite distant from the tree. Occasionally it forgets a hiding place and a seedling arises. In this way the tree becomes widely distributed. In certain localities *Bertholletia excelsa* is regarded as a commercial fruit-bearing tree, and the nuts within their carapaces are gathered from the ground. Production of Brazil nuts in orchards or plantations has failed because fertilization is dependent on wild bees.[229]

There are very few tree species in the Amazon jungle that reach 61 metres (200 feet) high. Among the emergents are *Dinizia excelsa*, a leguminous tree; the giant *Ceiba pentandra*, the silk-cotton tree already mentioned (page 85); and the widely distributed Brazil-nut tree.[230] There are other giant tree species but none that produces specimens so outstanding.

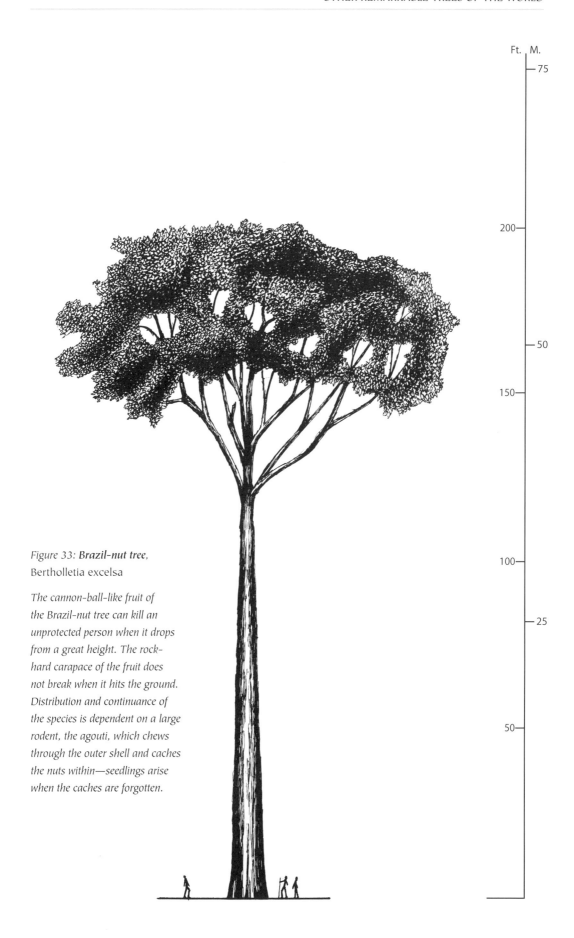

Ft. M.
— 75

200 —
— 50
150 —

100 —
— 25

50 —

Figure 33: **Brazil-nut tree**,
Bertholletia excelsa

*The cannon-ball-like fruit of
the Brazil-nut tree can kill an
unprotected person when it drops
from a great height. The rock-
hard carapace of the fruit does
not break when it hits the ground.
Distribution and continuance of
the species is dependent on a large
rodent, the agouti, which chews
through the outer shell and caches
the nuts within—seedlings arise
when the caches are forgotten.*

Wax palm

Ceroxylon andicola **and** *C. quindinense*

The tallest of the palm family are the wax palms of the northern Andes Mountains of South America. There are several species of these in this region. Two, *Ceroxylon andicola* (syn. *Alpinum*) and *C. quindinense*, represent the tallest palms in the world. Both are known to reach 61 metres (200 feet). Their trunks are quite slim, from 0.9 to 1.8 metres (3 to 6 feet) thick. They are found at very high elevations of up to 3,000 metres (10,000 feet), with outlying specimens as high as 4,085 metres (13,400 feet).[231]

These palms, with their large pinnate leaves, slim trunks and great height, present an eerie sight towering above the dwarf mountain vegetation. No wonder the first travellers to view them declared them to be the tallest trees in the world (Figure 34). Their leaves, stems and trunks are covered by a waxy coating that undoubtedly protects them from the chill temperatures of their mountain habitat, where they may encounter light frost and occasional snow.

One would expect that the tallest palms would grow in sheltered, lowland valleys with deep, fertile soil. Such trees would reach high, along with the lush vegetation there, to benefit from the rays of the sun and at the same time be protected from desiccating and damaging winds—but this is not so. The Andean wax palms appear to be a strange anomaly. It is of interest, however, that the second tallest palm species, the wanga, *Pigafetta filaris*, does grow under warm, junglelike conditions in the East Indian islands of Sulewesi, the Moluccas, and New Guinea. Specimens of it have been recorded growing 50 metres (164 feet) high.[232]The wanga, like the Andean palms, is a pinnate or feather-leaved palm. It has no wax sheathing.

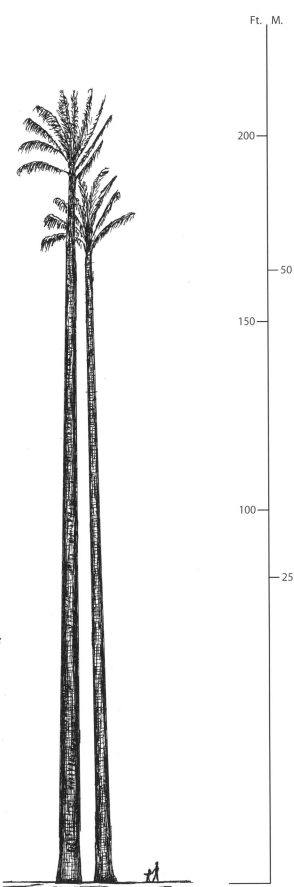

Ft. M.

— 200

— 50

— 150

— 100

— 25

*Figure 34: **Wax palm**,*
Ceroxylon andicola and C. *quindinense*

Wax palm, tallest of the palm family, are
found in the northern Andes Mountains
of South America. A waxy coating on
leaves, stems and trunks protects them
from the chill temperatures of their
mountain habitat, where they may
encounter light frost and occasional
snow.

ASIA

Coffin tree

Taiwania cryptomerioides **var.** *flousiana*

The natural history of China is intriguing because it is so diverse. Within this country's vast expanse are some of the most beautiful and wonderful forests on earth, along with deserts of the utmost desolation. China has everything in a topographical sense: hills, mountains, valleys, plains. Some are drenched with moisture and some are not, and some are heavily forested with a wide spectrum of tree types. Amid all this diversity, one might expect to find the world's tallest trees, but this is not the case. Far to the northwest in the Tien Shan range, Xinjiang Province, there are extensive forests of coniferous trees. One, known as Schrenk's spruce, *Picea schrenkiana*, grows tall in a splendid columnar form, but even the finest stands have few trees that greatly exceed 61 metres (200 feet) in height, though some have been found that reach 76.2 metres (250 feet).[233] In central China in the Qin Ling Mountains, Shaanxi Province, hills are clothed in places by a tall coniferous tree called Shensi fir, *Abies shensiensis*, but here again the maximum height does not exceed 76.2 metres (250 feet).[234] However, far to the southwest in Yunnan Province, with its many steep ridges and narrow valleys that lie within the influence of the monsoon rains, are forests of various kinds, and here is found China's tallest tree species, the coffin tree, *Taiwania cryptomerioides*, var. *flousiana*.

This tree was first described as living in Taiwan, hence its generic Latin name. However, in 1862 a very similar tree was found in Yunnan near the Burma border. This species has since been reported growing in the southern parts of Hubei and Guizhou provinces in localities where the climate is warm and humid. The Chinese and Taiwanese species are closely related; in fact the Chinese tree is but a geographical variant of that of Taiwan. The varietal term *flousiana* is drawn from the name of the first collector of the species, Fernande Flous, a French botanist. One tree of this kind was found to be 75 metres (246 feet) high and has been acclaimed the tallest tree in China.[235] The vernacular term "coffin" came to be applied because it was observed that the local Chinese preferred to use the planks from this tree for the manufacture of coffins.

The coffin tree when young has dense foliage with a spirelike top, but when aged it exhibits a bare trunk and its crown becomes more dome shaped. The trunk at a man's breast height can be as much as 12 feet (3.7 metres) thick.[236] The bark is red brown and peels in vertical strips. The needles are blue-green, narrow, prickly, awl-like and about 1.25 centimetres (0.5 inch) long; the cones are rounded and about 1.25 centimetres (0.5 inch) wide.

Himalayan or deodar cedar

Cedrus deodara

The hunt for giant trees is focussed on parts of the world where one would expect to find them. Prime localities offer moderate moisture, nearby hills or mountains to reduce the wind, and warmish temperatures. The Himalayas contain many deep, fertile valleys bathed with monsoon rains and moderate warmth. If not giants then at least tall trees would be expected. Such expectations, however, are only parsimoniously fulfilled.

The tallest, and about the largest, species of tree in the Himalayas is the deodar cedar, *Cedrus deodara*, indigenous to the western part of the mountain chain primarily at elevations of 1,220 to 3,000 metres (4,000 to 10,000 feet). It is a common tree in the Punjab of northwest India, northern Pakistan and northeast Afghanistan. Since it is an important timber tree it has been heavily exploited and many of the finest stands have disappeared. The tallest trees found now are at the most 61 metres (200 feet) high, but there is documented record of trees 76.2 metres (250 feet) high felled during the time of British imperial India 100 years ago. Some of these had trunks of impressive appearance such as 4.6 metres (15 feet) thick at a man's breast height and free of branches up to 24.4 metres (80 feet)[237] (note Figure 35). Large trees are thought to approach 1,000 years of age.[238]

There are four species of cedrus so closely related as to seem geographical variants. The best known is *Cedrus libani*, the famous Lebanon cedar of the eastern Mediterranean lands. In the Atlas Mountains of North Africa is the *C. atlantica*, and on the island of Cyprus, *C. brevifolia*. The tallest and most graceful, however, is that of the Himalayas. It is particularly attractive in its younger stages and is therefore much used as an ornamental. The timber of all cedrus species possesses a fragrant oil that aids in its preservation. The Himalayan cedar is especially rich in this.

The form of the mature Himalayan cedar is narrowly conical. The branches droop slightly and are arrayed with descending branch tips. The leading shoot is pronounced and droops also. The bark of mature trees is dark grey, fissured vertically into narrow ridges. The needles are long, up to 5 centimetres (2 inches), and are clustered in tufts on short spurs. The large barrel-shaped cones are 10 to 12 centimetres (4 to 5 inches) long and stand upright. They are first blue but change to brown as they ripen.

Figure 35: **Himalayan** or **deodar cedar**, Cedrus deodara

The Himalayan or deodar cedar is indigenous to the western part of the Himalayas, primarily at elevations of 1,220 to 3,000 metres (4,000 to 10,000 feet). There are documented records of trees 76.2 metres (250 feet) high felled during the time of British imperial India 100 years ago.

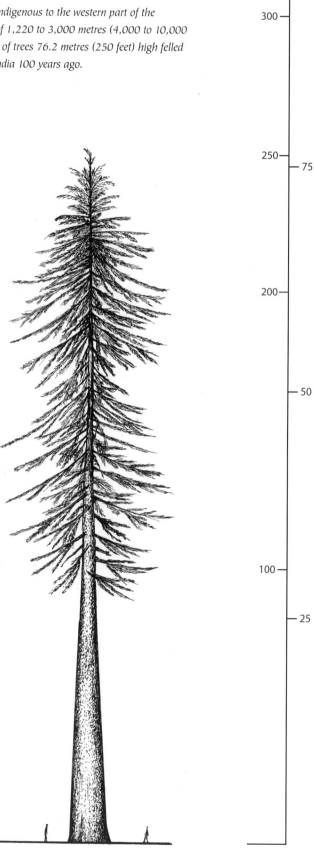

Ft. M.

300

250 — 75

200

— 50

100

— 25

Camphor tree

Cinnamomum camphora

The camphor tree is indigenous to Japan, Taiwan and southern China. In Japan there are a number of ancient monumental specimens. These are not found in the forests but are associated with Shinto shrines. They are protected as much as possible from the depredations of storms, earthquakes, tidal waves, insects, diseases and man. They are noted mainly for their gargantuan trunk size, although the canopy spread of mature younger trees can be spectacular.

The camphor tree is evergreen and prefers warmish climates. The leaves are simple with smooth margins, elliptical, 5 to 12 centimetres (2 to 5 inches) long and shiny. Just how long a camphor tree can live is not known but it is believed to be many centuries. Over that vast expanse of time it produces a huge, wide-spreading base structure.

The tree at Kamo, Kogochima, acclaimed as the biggest in Japan because of its trunk size, is 10.7 metres (35.1 feet) in diameter at ground level. The taper near the ground is rather acute, and yet its breast-height diameter is still 9.8 metres (32 feet). The trunk swellings extend up to a height of some 3 metres (10 feet), and here the trunk is 8.2 metres (27 feet) thick. Not far above this point the first branches jut out. Old records show that this tree was documented as a huge sacred tree in A.D. 1123. It is believed

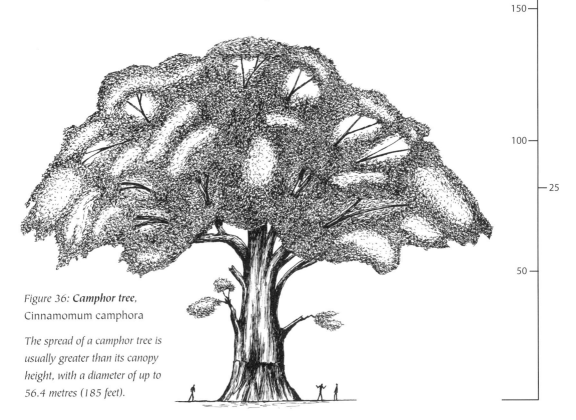

Figure 36: **Camphor tree**,
Cinnamomum camphora

The spread of a camphor tree is usually greater than its canopy height, with a diameter of up to 56.4 metres (185 feet).

to be at least two millennia old. It is in good health but its uppermost canopy shows the ravages of time. Its greatest height is no more than 24.4 metres (80 feet).[239]

The second largest tree in Japan is at Atami, Shizuoka. The trunk, although lumpy and full of contortions, is more or less upright and even-sized to where the branches begin. It has a breast-height diameter of 7.6 metres (25 feet) and is estimated to be 2,000 years old. A tree at Takeo, said to be the sixth largest in girth, has a breast-height trunk diameter of 6.4 metres (21 feet). It is completely hollow but judged to be 3,000 years old. Its canopy reaches to about 36.6 metres (120 feet) high. Although this tree has been damaged by storms over the centuries, it is still a most remarkable sight.[240] The greatest canopy height of these huge trees is 42.7 metres (140 feet), but the spread is usually greater, with a diameter up to 56.4 metres (185 feet) (see Figure 36).

Taiwan cypress

Chamaecyparis formosensis

Taiwan cypress is a cousin of Port Orford cedar (see page 48) but is known to have trees with trunks of much greater size. These super-large trees are exceedingly ancient and some are believed to have aged 3,000 years. The annual rings of one felled tree were counted to 2,700 years by a visiting botanist.[241] Such trees are to be found scattered in the mountainous north-central section of Taiwan Island. They are not to be confused with the Hinoki cypress, *Chamaecyparis obtusa* var. *formosana* (also designated *C. taiwanensis*), which is likewise native to Taiwan. This is a more handsome tree but is usually declared to be of less size than *C. formosensis*.

In 1907, world traveller and tree hunter H.J. Elwes was shown a Taiwan cypress that was 49.4 metres (162 feet) tall with a bole thickness of 5.8 metres (19 feet). He said that specimens with trunks up to 7.6 metres (25 feet) thick had been reported.[242] Indeed, a tree now standing at Ta-hsue-shan, near the centre of the island, is said to have a breast-height trunk diameter of 8.7 metres (28.5 feet), and several other trees in that central zone are not greatly less (Figure 37).[243] Such thickness of trunk is greater than the largest red cedar, placing these trees in the same bole-size category as the largest giant sequoias of California.

The trunks of these ancient trees are markedly ridged, and the fibrous bark is a rich red brown, adding to their attractiveness. The tree as a whole is not outstandingly aesthetic. It does not have a well-formed, shapely head of foliage and the sprays of flattened needles may be bronzed. It is not extremely tall, about 70 metres (230 feet) at the most, and this is a historical record. The finest stands have long since been logged out. The wood is exceptionally choice, fine grained, rich pink in colour and pleasantly scented. It is also extremely durable.

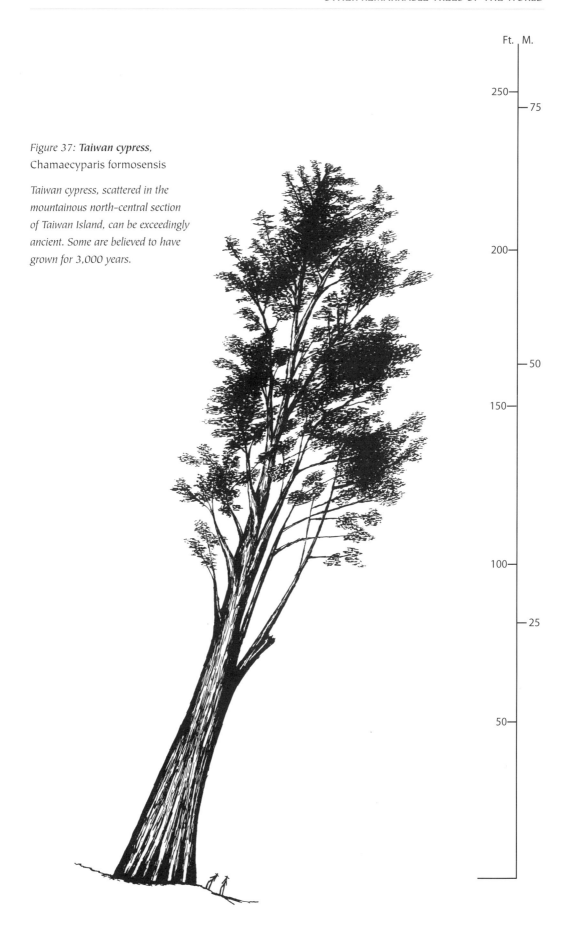

Ft.   M.

Figure 37: **Taiwan cypress**,
Chamaecyparis formosensis

Taiwan cypress, scattered in the
mountainous north-central section
of Taiwan Island, can be exceedingly
ancient. Some are believed to have
grown for 3,000 years.

Trees of Lesser Stature, British Columbia and the Pacific Northwest

Western hemlock

Tsuga heterophylla

Although not in the category of the giant Douglas-fir, Sitka spruce and western red cedar of the coastal forests of Pacific North America, western hemlock would be very noticeable in most forests elsewhere. A specimen in British Columbia just north of the city of Vancouver has recently been measured with a bole 3 metres (9.5 feet) thick at a man's breast height.[244] Another tree in the same locality was 2.7 metres (9 feet) in bole diameter. The larger tree was 45.7 metres (150 feet) high despite a blown-off top. A tree in the Tahsish Valley, northern Vancouver Island, upheld its nodding head 75.6 metres (248 feet) above the ground (Figure 38). This tree was close knit with its peers and remarkably slim, with a trunk only 1 metre (3.3 feet) thick at breast height.[245] These are records and they are especially significant as there are some mighty western hemlock trees in the vast expanses of the Olympic Park, Washington State, where this species does well and has never suffered from the consequences of logging. Two of the giant trees there have breast-height trunk diameters just under 2.7 metres (9 feet). A slim tree, 73.5 metres (241 feet) high, close to the height of the Tahsish Tree was found in the Hoh Valley of the park.[246] A hemlock in Prairie Creek Redwood State Park in California was measured at 78 metres (256 feet) but it has since fallen.

When walking through a forest where the giant Douglas-fir, Sitka spruce and western red cedar grow, western hemlock appears low on the scale of dominance, but a close look reveals a plentiful population comprising a substantial amount of foliage so thick that its shade prevents the establishment of most other tree species. The corollary to this is that the modest western hemlock does in fact play an important role in the forests of the Pacific Coast.

In most localities it represents the climax species. If the forest never suffers an outright disruption, such as fire, blowdown, or earthquake, the succession of the tree species would terminate as hemlock. This species is highly shade tolerant and able to carry on successfully beneath its giant cohabitants while it waits for a place in the sun.

Although it is exceedingly well adapted to shade and is therefore largely protected from turbulence, western hemlock does not suffer greatly from wind because the flexible cellular structure of its wood gives it great resilience. This feature is exemplified in the pendent leader and drooping branches. It is a graceful tree, and its small needles and cones add to this impression.

It is only recently that people have realized western hemlock can live to a great age. A grove in Cypress Park near Vancouver was found to have trees exceeding 900 years old, and a stump in the Caren Range, Coast Mountains, British Columbia, showed 1,238 growth rings.[247]

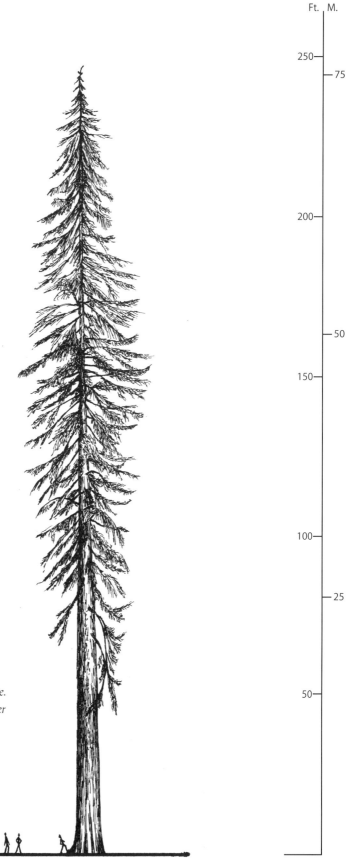

Ft. M.

250 — 75

200

— 50

150

100

— 25

50

Figure 38: **Western hemlock,**
Tsuga heterophylla

*Western hemlock can live to a great age.
A grove in Cypress Park near Vancouver
was found to have trees exceeding 900
years old and a stump in the Caren
Range of British Columbia showed
1,238 growth rings.*

Western hemlock thrives over a considerable range. It can be found along the coast west of the coastal and Cascade mountains from southeast Alaska to northern California. There is also an inland distribution through southeastern British Columbia and northern Idaho, but the trees there are shorter than those near the coast.

Grand fir

Abies grandis

According to early accounts, grand fir was once a grander tree than it is now. Since the largest trees were near the coast along lowland streams, they were logged first. Old records give 91.5 metres (300 feet) as the maximum height,[248] but there is no recent authoritative measurement of such a tall tree.

The biggest grand fir standing today is the Chilliwack Giant, named after a nearby town in coastal British Columbia. Its trunk is 2.2 metres (7.1 feet) in breast-height diameter.[249] The tallest tree is in the Glacial Park Wilderness, Washington State, and it reaches up 81.4 metres (267 feet).[250] A 79.9-metre (262-foot) specimen is attested to live or to have lived on Vancouver Island, where there are many fine groves of this species.[251]

Grand fir is possibly the most rapidly growing of all the giant conifers and has been known to reach a height of 42.7 metres (140 feet) in 50 years. It is not a long-lived tree, 300 years being its maximum age.[252] It thrives best where the plentiful West Coast precipitation is somewhat reduced by rain shadow effect. The fact that it prefers low elevations has given it its other common name of lowland fir.

Grand fir is a handsome tree with attractive splays of broad, flat, glossy needles about 5 centimetres (2 inches) long and all more or less on the same plane. It is a narrow-crowned tree. In dense forest its bole may be clear of branches for more than 30 metres (100 feet) but if open grown the branches are retained, even those close to the ground. One peculiarity is that on mature trees the top may be quite rounded (Figure 39). This is caused by the continued growth of the top side branches after the leader slows its upward thrust.

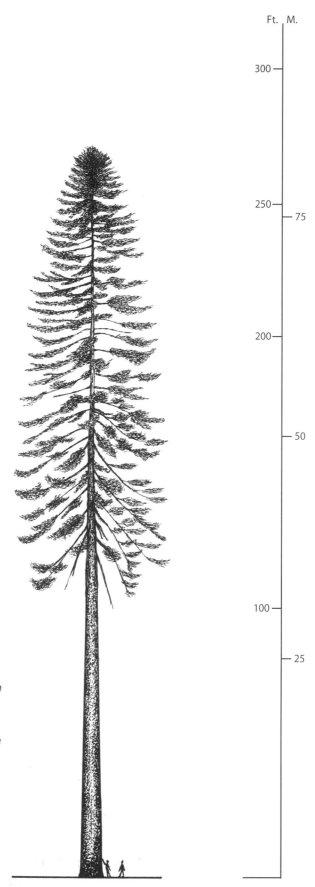

Ft. M.

300

250 — 75

200

— 50

100

— 25

*Figure 39: **Grand fir**,*
Abies grandis

*Although it is not a long-lived tree, 300
years being its maximum age, grand fir
is possibly the most rapidly growing of
all the giant conifers. It has been known
to reach a height of 42.7 metres (140
feet) in only 50 years.*

Amabilis or Pacific silver fir

Abies amabilis

Silver fir is called amabilis in British Columbia after the specific part of its scientific name. Since its normal habitat is above 300 metres (1,000 feet) elevation, its destruction by logging was delayed and many of the finest stands remained until quite recent times. Consequently most records of champion amabilis trees are quite modern rather than from long ago as they are in the case of Douglas-fir and other lowland timber species. Amabilis ranges from the southern extremity of Alaska to southern Oregon. It is a highly shade tolerant species and prefers cool, moist environments. Under such conditions, like western hemlock, *Tsuga heterophylla*, it assumes the role of a climax species. There it can live for a very long time, approaching 1,000 years.[253]

Amabilis fir is a princely tree, shapely and spirelike with downward sloping branches turning up at the ends. The bark is a light grey. The foliage is dense and lustrous. The needles are rather short, about 3.8 centimetres (1.5 inches) long. Their upper side is dark green but the underside is a silvery white and it is this that has given the tree the name silver fir. The cones are large, up to 15 centimetres (6 inches) long. They stand upright on the higher branches and have a purplish colour that makes them quite conspicuous.

The largest tree found so far in British Columbia is in Cypress Provincial Park. It is 47 metres (154 feet) to a damaged top, with a bole diameter of 2.3 metres (7.6 feet). According to big-tree coordinator Robert Van Pelt, this tree is the biggest (on volume basis) living amabilis fir known.[254] To the south, in Olympic National Forest, Van Pelt measured a larger tree that only recently blew down due to logging nearby. This was 63.4 metres (208 feet) high with a breast-height trunk diameter of 2.4 metres (7.8 feet). The tallest living tree measured in this area by Van Pelt is 71.3 metres (234 feet) high.[255] Figure 40 shows the form of a mature tree. Note the sloping branches upturned at the ends.

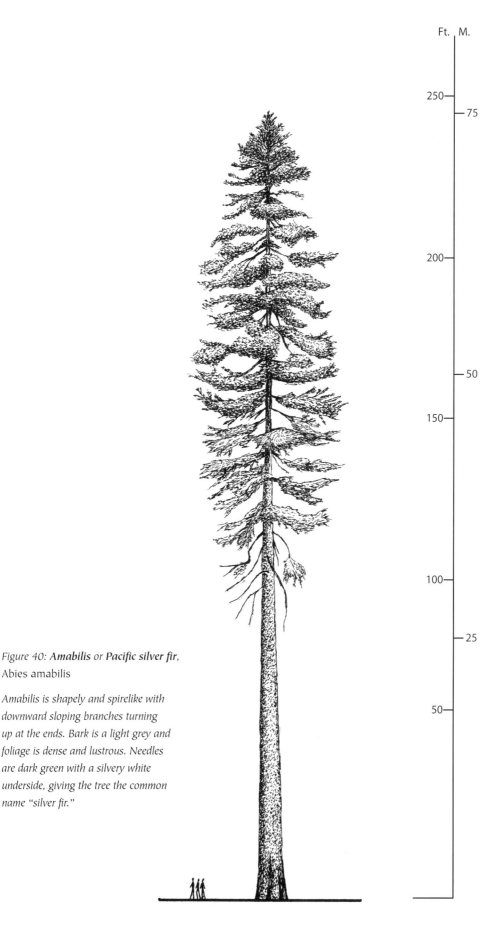

Ft.   M.

250 — 75

200 — 50

150 —

100 — 25

50 —

*Figure 40: **Amabilis** or **Pacific silver fir**,* Abies amabilis

Amabilis is shapely and spirelike with downward sloping branches turning up at the ends. Bark is a light grey and foliage is dense and lustrous. Needles are dark green with a silvery white underside, giving the tree the common name "silver fir."

Western larch

Larix occidentalis

Western larch is a tree of the mountains that thrives in the valleys and on slopes where there is sufficient moisture for substantial growth. Its range takes in southeastern British Columbia, northeastern Washington, northern Idaho and northwestern Montana plus outlying mountainous areas including the Cascades. It is a distinctive tree with horizontal branches that are surprisingly short. The trunk is shaftlike and can be clear for 30 metres (100 feet). Its slim form can make it appear taller than it actually is. It is the tallest of all the world's species of larch including the giant of Europe, *L. decidua*. Unlike most conifers it is deciduous, so in summer it is noticeable for its light, lustrous green foliage and in winter for its bareness. Its bark is a rich reddish brown and is composed of oblong plates separated by rather deep furrows. On mature trees the bark can be 15 centimetres (6 inches) thick near the base. The tree can live for a very long time; one fallen tree showed 915 growth rings.[256]

Western larch, like Douglas-fir, produces valuable timber. It has therefore been intensively logged and all the biggest and finest trees are gone. Currently the tallest tree that has been found is 58.5 metres (192 feet) high, while the biggest in thickness of trunk is 2.2 metres (7.2 feet),[257] but reports from the middle of the last century give 64 metres (210 feet) and 2.4 metres (8 feet) as the greatest dimensions.[258] From 1904 there is an account of a tree in Montana 71 metres (233 feet) high, which was then declared the tallest of the species in the state.[259] Figure 41 shows the exceptionally short branches and general slimness of the tree.

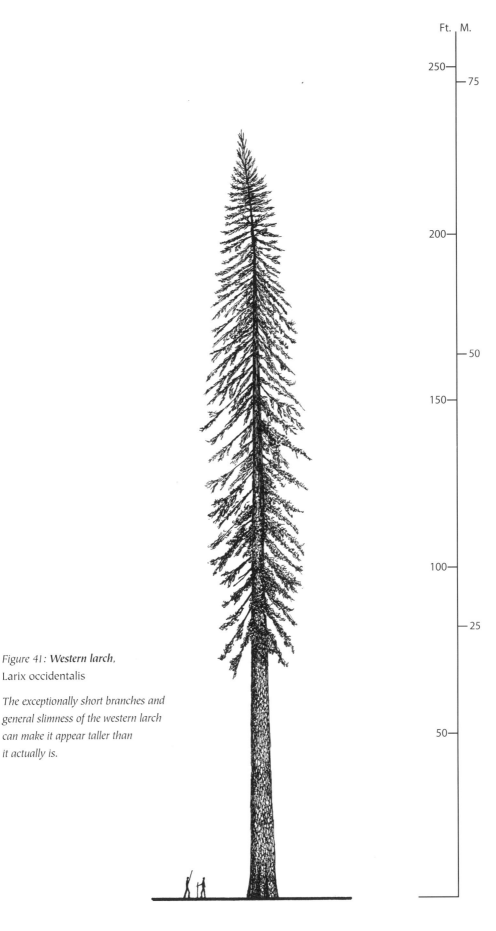

Figure 41: **Western larch**,
Larix occidentalis

The exceptionally short branches and
general slimness of the western larch
can make it appear taller than
it actually is.

Englemann spruce

Picea englemanni

Like many subalpine tree species, Englemann spruce has a thin, spirelike crown. Thus, although small, it can reach a fair height. This tree is supremely adapted to the cold. In some mountain areas it can thrive at elevations as high as 3,660 metres (12,000 feet). Yet it can also be found at quite low elevations where cold air drains and accumulates. In such locations it is protected from the harsh mountain storms and the soils are richer, promoting better growth. This is where the tallest specimens grow. Big-tree hunter Robert Van Pelt came upon one on the lower slopes of the Cascade Mountains that measured 64.9 metres (213 feet),[279] and he was surprised that this species could be so tall. Unfortunately it died soon after this event. Van Pelt continued his searching and in 1996 found another tall Englemann spruce in a pass of the Cascades. This tree's slim, lofty spire towered 68 metres (223 feet) high.[280] It was extraordinarily slim, having a breast-height trunk diameter of just 1.7 metres (5.5 feet). Other tall and super-large Englemann spruces have been located under similar conditions. One tree in British Columbia's Coast Mountains has a bole diameter of 2.2 metres (7.2 feet).[281] This tree was observed many years ago by the late Randy Stoltmann, British Columbia's peerless big-tree hunter.

The form of an Englemann spruce is narrow with dense, slightly drooping branches that shed the heavy winter snows. The foliage is an attractive dark blue-green, and because it is tolerant to shade it is retained well down the bole. The bark is a reddish brown with loosely attached scales. It is thin, about 1.3 centimetres (0.5 inches) thick. The tree is long lived, surviving more than 500 years, with one specimen showing 660 growth rings.[282]

The subalpine nature of Englemann spruce largely determines its range. It is well distributed through the mountainous southern half of British Columbia, then along the Rocky Mountains south to Colorado, with isolated outriders beyond. A protrusion of it follows the eastern slopes of the Cascade Mountains to southern Oregon.

Bigleaf or broadleaf maple

Acer macrophyllum

The bigleaf maple is the largest of over 200 species of maple in the world. It not only has the largest all around size, but is bigger in practically every respect. The leaves are enormous, commonly measuring 30.5 centimetres (1 foot) in width and length, with exceptional leaves having a width of 61 centimetres (2 feet). The leaf stalks are very stout and strong and can be 30.5 centimetres (1 foot) long. A tree near the town of Hemlock, Oregon, has a breast-height bole diameter of 3.6 metres (11.8 feet) and a crown span of 31.1 metres (102 feet),[260] while a forest-grown specimen in the Mount Baker National Forest, Washington State, reaches 48.2 metres (158 feet) high.[261] There are also exceptional trees in British Columbia that are very near to these dimensions.

The next largest maple species in the world is *A. velutinum*, commonly called velvet maple, which is native to the eastern Caucasus Mountains and northwest Iran. It is known to soar upward to 36.6 metres (120 feet) or more and to have leaves 30.5 centimetres (1 foot) wide. Grown in the open it can be a fully rounded, domed tree with a trunk 3 metres (10 feet) thick.[262] Europe's largest maple is known as the sycamore, *A. pseudoplatanus*. In the British Isles it is referred to as the great maple, a very good name for it. Trees of this species can reach 40.2 metres (132 feet) high, have a trunk 2.7 metres (8.8 feet) thick and a crown span of 24.4 metres (80 feet).[263] There is, however, one feature in which bigleaf maple does not excel, and that is length of life. Evidence indicates that 250 to 300 years is the ultimate age.[264] This compares to 500 years or more attained by the European sycamore[265] or the various species of maple of eastern North America.[266]

When bigleaf maple has a chance to grow in the open it branches out fairly low down and forms a magnificent rounded crown of dark green foliage, but when forest grown it forms a tall bole clear of branches for as much as 24.4 metres (80 feet). The crown is narrow, reduced and held much higher than that of an open-grown tree (compare Figures 42 and 43). In cases like this, especially if hemmed in by tall-growing conifers, it may lose out in the battle for light and slowly succumb.

The bark of a mature bigleaf maple is a greyish brown, shallowly fissured into narrow ridges. It is thin, usually not more than 1.3 centimetres (0.5 inch) thick. All parts of the tree, such as buds, leaves and twigs, grow in pairs so that each is opposite the other. In the autumn the leaves turn a bright orange yellow, but the display is poor if the weather is inclement.

In those areas where there is much moisture and fog, the bole and branches of bigleaf maple become beset with lichens, mosses, liverworts and ferns. Large trees may accumulate a tonne of such plants along with other debris. It has recently been found that this is not a disadvantage to the tree but may be an asset. Such plants build up a soil of their own, and the tree produces small roots from its stems that penetrate the soil and obtain nourishment, especially nitrogen gathered by certain of these epiphytic plants. Bigleaf maple is a soil-building and soil-improving species that enriches the site on which it grows. It has a shallow, wide-spreading root system.

The maximum sizes bigleaf maple attains have been described, but the normal size is about 30.5 metres (100 feet) tall, 21.3 metres (70 feet) in width of crown, with a bole 0.9 to 1.2 metres (3 or 4 feet) in diameter. It thrives scattered among other tree species from near the north end of Vancouver Island and the adjacent mainland coast southward through Washington and Oregon to northern California, but usually not more than 160 kilometres (100 miles) from the ocean.

Almost all the world's species of maple are in the northern hemisphere. There are 13 in North America, including three in the northwest of this continent. Bigleaf maple is one of the latter three. Its two associates—vine maple, A. circinatum, and Douglas maple, A. glabrum—are of much smaller form. There is no interbreeding of the northwest species.

*Figure 42 : **Bigleaf** or **broadleaf maple**, Acer macrophyllum*

When bigleaf maple has a chance to grow in the open it branches out fairly low down and forms a magnificent rounded crown of dark green foliage.

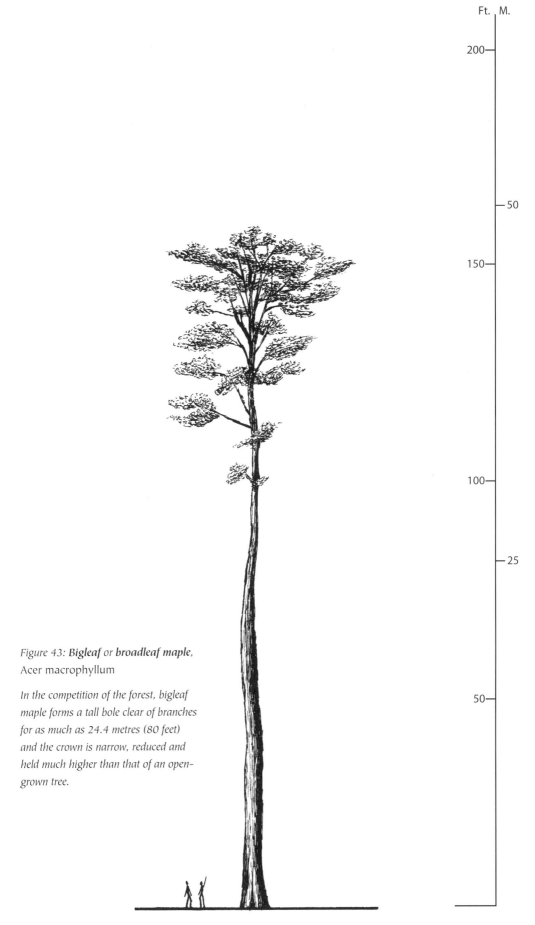

Ft. M.

200—

—50

150—

100—

—25

50—

Figure 43: **Bigleaf** or **broadleaf maple**, Acer macrophyllum

In the competition of the forest, bigleaf maple forms a tall bole clear of branches for as much as 24.4 metres (80 feet) and the crown is narrow, reduced and held much higher than that of an open-grown tree.

Other Trees of Lesser Stature, the World

Incense cedar

Calocedrus decurrens

Incense cedar is found in the same general area as Port Orford cedar but with a more extended range inland and much farther south following the Sierra Nevada, even as far as the Baja Peninsula of northern Mexico. This tree is outstanding wherever seen in the forest but lacks the commanding size of the Port Orford cedar. The greatest measurements reported are a height of 69.8 metres (229 feet) and a bole thickness of 4.3 metres (14 feet).[267] These maximum dimensions are from different trees. The largest now living is known as the Devil's Canyon Colossus and it is 50.3 metres (165 feet) high with a trunk diameter of 3.8 metres (12.4 feet).[268] Figure 44 shows the greatest dimensions ever measured for an incense cedar.

The bark of incense cedar is a dark tawny brown, stringy and fibrous, about 15 centimetres (6 inches) thick and deeply ridged. The trunk of old trees is fluted and may be buttressed near the base. A peculiarity affecting the general form of the tree, especially mature and older ones, is that the branches develop thickened elbows as they leave the trunk and this directs the boughs upward at awkward angles, giving the crown a craggy appearance, as Figure 44 demonstrates. Incense cedar is long lived and may reach ages of 800 to nearly 1,000 years.[269]

Jeffrey pine

Pinus jeffreyi

Jeffrey pine is a close relative of ponderosa pine (see page 42) Both have needles in bunches of three, but the needles of Jeffrey pine are longer, 18 to 28 centimetres (7 to 11 inches), and bear a bluish tinge. The huge cones, 13 to 30 centimetres (5 to 12 inches) long, are much larger than those of ponderosa. The bark structure is similar except that the bark of Jeffrey pine is a darker red. The general outline or form of the trees is different. Jeffrey pine is on the whole a more thickset, stalwart tree with rather wide-spreading branches. The crown of a mature tree tends to be open and quite rounded, while that of a ponderosa is more pyramidal. Jeffrey is generally a shorter tree and thus may appear smaller, but this is not always so. For volume of wood, the record goes to Jeffrey pine.[270]

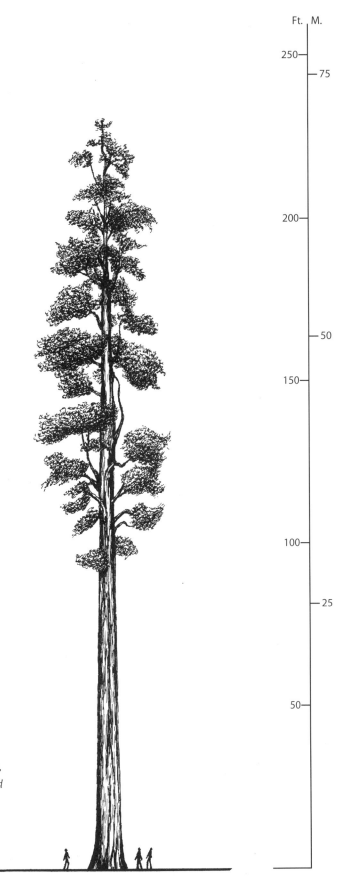

Ft. M.

250—
——75

200—

——50
150—

100—
——25

50—

Figure 44: **Incense cedar**,
Calocedrus decurrens

The bark of incense cedar is a dark
tawny brown, fibrous and and deeply
ridged. The trunk of old trees is fluted
and may be buttressed near the base.
In mature trees, the branches develop
thickened elbows as they leave the trunk,
directing the boughs upward at awkward
angles, giving the crown a craggy
appearance.

One size requirement for a big tree in this study is that a species must have a member or members at least 61 metres (200 feet) tall. This is very seldom attained by Jeffrey pine, and Robert Van Pelt in his search for the giants of each tree species reports measuring only one Jeffrey pine that reached a height of 63.1 metres (207 feet).[271] Other reports indicate that there is a good possibility this pine does occasionally surpass the 61-metre (200-foot) height.[272] One tree that was measured had a bole diameter of as much as 2.5 metres (8.1 feet) at breast height.[273]

The evidence is that Jeffrey pine does not quite equal the ages attained by ponderosa. Nevertheless it is long lived—at least 500 years. A tree 600 years old was felled in the Stanislaus Forest, California.[274] Its distribution is rather limited, being largely confined to the Sierra Nevada range with outlying areas in southwest Oregon, northwest California and far to the south in the northern Baja Peninsula, Mexico.

Red and white firs

Abies magnifica **and** *A. concolor*

Red and white firs grow from mid-Oregon to well into California. Their profiles are much the same: single-stemmed trees with shortish branches and a pyramidal crown when young but domed when old. This narrow, spirelike form is highly suited to shed the heavy winter snows of the mountain environment. In general, red fir is the larger tree, but the white fir does very well for itself. Maximum-sized specimens of each are similar. A red fir has been found that has a breast-height bole diameter of 3 metres (9.7 feet),[275] while the largest white fir known, one that is dead and fallen, is 2.7 metres (8.9 feet) thick at this point.[276] Likewise, the tallest red fir measured out at 76.8 metres (252 feet),[277] with a white specimen scaling 75 metres (246 feet) high.[278] A factor adding to the majesty of red fir is its bark, which on mature trees is a rich reddish brown, while that of white fir is a lacklustre grey. The bark of both trees is 8 to 13 centimetres (3 to 5 inches) thick and deeply ridged in crisscross fashion.

These species of fir, however, differ markedly in their choice of habitat. The red fir flourishes best at elevations of 1,830 to 2,750 metres (6,000 to 9,000 feet), while the finest stands of the white occur rather lower, between 1,220 and 2,130 metres (4,000 and 7,000 feet). The maximum ages attained are similar at about 500 years.

There are two varieties or subspecies of red fir: *Abies magnifica* var. *magnifica* and *A. m.* var. *shastensis*. In form they are indistinguishable and they are treated here as one. The difference is mainly in the appearance or non-appearance of the cone bracts. There are also two varieties of white fir: *Abies concolor* var. *concolor* and *A. c.* var. *lowiana*. Here the difference is in the arrangement of stomata in the needles, but there is also a difference in tree height attained. *A. concolor* var. *lowiana* is largely confined to the Yosemite Valley, where it grows tall. It is chosen to represent the species described here.

Korean spruce

Picea koraiensis

The coffin tree, *Taiwania cryptomerioides*, previously described (see page 102) and declared the tallest tree in China, is, however, not the tallest in Asia. The prize in this case goes to a spruce in Korea, *Picea koraiensis*, where one specimen stood 79.9 metres (262 feet) high.[283] This tree usually goes under the name of Korean spruce and is not to be confused with other closely related spruces, such as Koyama, of the nursery trade. These are also indigenous to Korea or nearby states, but none grows to an impressive height or size.

Saman

Albitzia saman

Much has been said in these pages about how tall trees can grow, how big their trunks can get, how far up their trunks can reach before branching out. These are all important features that outline a tree's form or silhouette, but less has been said about branch spread, which also determines tree shape. Certain trees have mighty branches that, rather than extending upward, jut out horizontally for virtually all their length. Such trees exhibit a tremendous spread of verdure and certain species are noted for this. One in particular is the saman or raintree, botanically termed *Albitzia saman* (syn. *Pithecellobium saman*). Other vernacular names for the saman are samang or monkey-pod, depending on where it is grown. It is a warmth-loving tree, native to Central America and northern South America and much favoured as a shade tree, for which reason it can be found in many subtropical countries of the world. It is a legume, a mimosa, with leaves pinnately compound and leaflets small and delicate, seemingly incongruous for such a large tree. When in flower it is very beautiful, with bright red blossoms.

One reason it is called raintree may be because the grass beneath it remains green and reasonably fresh during drought. This is due to two peculiarities. First, it has the habit of folding or closing its leaves with the coming of darkness or the twilight that accompanies a shower so that rain, and even dew, passes through and refreshes the grass beneath. Another explanation is that sucking insects attack the leaves and exude droplets of moisture, which fall to the ground.

The term monkey-pod refers to its fruiting bodies, which are podlike, 10 to 13 centimetres (4 to 5 inches) long and somewhat curved. The seeds within are edible and have a licorice flavour much relished by monkeys and children.

The raintree is favoured as a shade tree because of its exceptionally wide canopy, especially if open grown as in a park. The configuration of such a tree is a huge dome-like mass of foliage upheld by a single trunk. The tree can be evergreen or deciduous depending largely upon location. In very warm equatorial regions it will be evergreen, in cooler regions deciduous.

Several of these trees have grown to such voluminous proportions as to gain worldwide renown. There is, or was, the great samang tree in the valley of the Araqua River, Venezuela, first reported on in the 1500s. It is not known now if this tree remains. Humboldt visited it about 1800 and a measurement was made late in that century. The trunk was rather less than 3 metres (10 feet) thick and extended upward for 18.3 metres (60 feet). The branch spread, however, was spectacular, averaging (on the basis of circumference) 55 metres (180 feet) in diameter.[284] Travellers have described how noticeable its dome of dark green foliage was from miles off as they descended into the valley of the Araqua River. Up close this tree was beautiful, made so by orchids and other flowering plants that hung from its boughs.

Another well-publicized tree is on the island of Tobago near Trinidad. This is believed to be rather young, not greatly over 100 years old. When last measured, about 1990, it had a trunk 2.4 metres (8 feet) in diameter. The total height of the tree was 44.8 metres (147 feet) with a crown spread, based on a circumference measurement, of 57 metres (187 feet).[285]

In this matter of branch spread there seems nothing that exceeds the raintree. Some species, such as oak, are known to extend their branches horizontally for great distances. The Sun Oak in Sussex, England, a common or English oak, *Quercus robur*, has branches that stretch either side of its trunk for 18.3 metres (60 feet), giving a span of more than 36.6 metres (120 feet), but this is considerably less than that attained by the raintree.[286] However, John Evelyn in the publication "Silva," based on his research conducted in the 1660s, gives the measurements of a giant oak in Worksop Park, England, that spanned 55 metres (180 feet) from bough end to bough end.[287] The canopy of a giant camphor tree, *Cinnamomum camphora*, in Japan is said to span at least this (see page 105). Thomas Pakenham recounts measuring a common oak in central Ireland that had a branch jutting out parallel to the ground for 27.4 metres (90 feet).[288]

The Angel Oak in South Carolina has a limb spread of 46 metres (151 feet), while another at Hahnville, Louisiana, is said to have one of 51.8 metres (170 feet),[289] but it must be recognized that these are bough spreads at their extreme, whereas the data for the raintree is based on an average span of innumerable branches.

A tree with an enormous trunk size would be expected to support a remarkable spread of foliage. For instance, the monstrous Montezuma cypress, *Taxodium mucronatum*, at El Tule near Oaxaca, Mexico, has a trunk diameter of 11.6 metres (38 feet). It does, indeed, have an unusual span of foliage but really no record, having a total spread of 45.7 metres (150 feet) including the distance taken up by the trunk.[290] The chestnut tree, *Castanea sativa*, on Mount Etna, island of Sicily, known as the Chestnut Tree of 100 Horses (see page 58) had in its prime a bole diameter of over 18.3 metres (60 feet), yet its branch spread averaged no more than 39.6 metres (130 feet).[291] Some specimens of the baobab tree, *Adansonia digitata*, of Africa have a trunk diameter of 12.2 metres (40 feet) but branch spreads do not exceed 45.7 metres (150 feet).[292]

There is a yew tree, *Taxus baccata*, at Whittinghame, East Lothian, Scotland, that has an exceptional span of foliage that touches the ground, and from a distance the tree appears as a vast green mound. Its total spread of branches is 30 metres (95 feet).[293] A noted jungle tree, *Ceiba pentandra*, of Central and South America and Africa, sometimes throws out huge elongated side branches. One such tree in the town of Palin, Guatemala, has a branch span of 47.3 metres (155 feet).[294] Robert Van Pelt recounts measuring a tree of this species on Barro Colorado Island, Panama, that had an average crown span of 61.3 metres (201 feet), thus exceeding that of the raintree.[295]

Great spans of foliage have been proclaimed for the oriental plane tree, *Platanus orientalis*. However, such statements are not based on actual branch spread but on the fact that one or more of the tree's larger branches may extend far out and in time sag to the ground where, at contact, roots form that revitalize the branch beyond. This of course leads to further expansion.[296] However, such growths do not reflect the tree's ability to support an exceptionally wide-spreading crown. There are several other tree species that behave similarly, including the banyan tree, *Ficus benghalensis*, of India.

There is no tree in British Columbia that has a branch spread anywhere near those recounted above. The closest would be the giant bigleaf maple, *Acer macrophyllum*, and no specimen of it, even when open grown, reaches such proportions width-wise.

Palmyra palm

sp. *Borassus aethiopium*

Of all the palm species, that with the thickest trunk appears to be a variety of *Borassus aethiopium*. This is a Palmyra palm, a fan palm found in Africa from Egypt to as far south as Zimbabwe. Specimens along the flood plain of rivers in Tanzania grow to a truly colossal size. Some are as much as 2.1 metres (7 feet) thick at breast height with a bulge or belly, the ventricosity, much broader higher up. One report gives a bole 3.4 metres (11 feet) thick at breast height that reaches a height of at least 30.5 metres (100 feet)[297] (Figure 45). The Chilean wine palm, *Jubaea chilensis* (syn. *spectabilis*), a feather-leaved palm, seems next in having a broad trunk. Some mature plants of this species have boles 2 metres (6.5 feet) thick and are 25.9 metres (85 feet) high, including their pinnate fronds.[298]

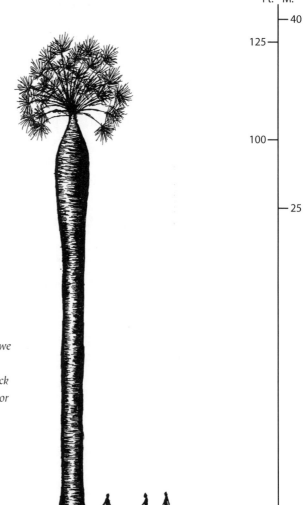

*Figure 45: **Palmyra palm**, sp.* Borassus aethiopium

The Palmyra palm is found in Africa from Egypt to as far south as Zimbabwe and can grow to a truly colossal size—as big as 2.1 metres (7 feet) thick at breast height with a broader bulge or belly higher up.

Ft. M.

125

100

The Tallest, Largest and Oldest Trees

It was photosynthesis, that magical and wonderful physiochemical process introduced by living cells, that brought about the buildup of great size in plants. There was an advantage in being tall and able to reach for the light, that source of power. Even 300 million years ago there were tall races of plants. Some ancient forms of clubmoss, the lepidodendron, grew 45 metres (150 feet) high. As time went on plants became taller and larger with more intricate structuring to support the upward thrust. Finally, huge sequoia-like trees evolved, depending upon their enormity to attain great height. Still later, trees such as the eucalypts and pseudotsugas developed specialized cells in their wood for support rather than relying on sheer bulk to gain superior height.

Unfortunately we cannot now say what height or size the world's existing or recently existing great trees did attain, as many of the best have been destroyed by industrial man with few measurements having been made. We must rely, therefore, in part on what skimpy determinations were obtained when the forests were in their pristine state and accept those measurements that we believe were gathered in truthful fashion.

The following charts and table summarize what has been outlined in the text. In respect to the greatest height ever attained by these mighty trees (Chart 1), the lead is taken by the mountain ash of Australia. Even the measurement given here for this tree is that of a specimen with a missing top. Note that the present tallest known specimens of the various species are almost always less than measurements made when the forests were in their virgin state, that is, before the ravages wrought upon them by industrial man (compare Charts 1 and 2). The reason why there is no height reduction over time for Sitka spruce, manna gum and alpine ash (Chart 1) is that the tallest specimens of these were only recently discovered and they were soon protected by park establishments—all credit to the altruistic sense of man! Most of the height reductions (Chart 2) are due to logging or settlement, though some have been indirectly caused by the opening of forests to the harmful effects of wind. Note also that the maximum height of British Columbia's outstandingly tall tree, Douglas-fir, has been reduced by more than 20 percent; this in contrast to that of Sitka spruce.

The wanton destruction of the forests in British Columbia has resulted in two artificial scenarios. First, the tallest tree standing in the world today is a coast redwood (Chart 1). How this came about has been described (see page 32). The tallest tree now standing in Canada is a Sitka spruce. This is in part due to the fact that Sitka spruce thrives best in areas not attractive to man's settlement and therefore did not suffer the early despoliation experienced by some other species of tree, particularly Douglas-fir. Also, by the time the finest stands of Sitka spruce were found, consciousness of what was happening to our forests had become aroused. Here we should mention the late Randy Stoltmann, that courageous and determined young man who took up the fight against the giant and rapacious timber companies.

British Columbia is a place of tall trees, but it does not boast specimens with the thickest trunks. For example, the province has no representative of such a tree in Chart 3. The greatest diameter of a standing tree in BC is the Cheewhat Lake Cedar on the southwest coast of Vancouver Island with a breast-height trunk diameter of 5.9 metres

(19.2 feet). No tree of times past is known to be much larger. There is no breast-height measurement of the trunk of the Sointula Cedar, a vast red cedar cut down in 1923 on Montcalm Island off the northeast coast of Vancouver Island, but what can be gathered from other measurements and photographs of it suggests it may have been a bit larger, perhaps with a trunk 6.7 to 7 metres (22 to 23 feet) thick (page 20).

Table 1 summarizes the greatest ages trees have been found to attain. Much of the data is approximate but it is the best available. There are many difficulties in determining the age of trees, especially when over 1,000 years old. For some, such as Douglas-fir, the maximum age attainable is rather definitely known as a considerable number of determinations have been made on patriarchal specimens, but this is not always the case with other species of giant trees of British Columbia. Numerous western red cedars of the northwest coast of North America have had their annual growth rings counted but not the biggest because they are hollow. Moreover, huge cedars that have grown along the southwest coast of Vancouver Island, where the temperatures are always cool even in summer, produce growth rings exceedingly close together. The rings of these have never been counted so it is likely such giant trees as the Cheewhat Lake Cedar do surpass 2,000 years of age. Likewise, the maximum ages of certain yellow cedars have very possibly exceeded 2,000 years. The ages attained by other indigenous trees of British Columbia are less. No tree of Sitka spruce has been found to be 1,000 years old, although trees of the smaller western hemlock are known to surpass 1,200 annual growth rings.

For trees that have lived for several millennia we must go elsewhere than British Columbia. The most ancient of the giant or Sierra sequoias have been found to be 3,500 years old, but it has been determined that several smaller species of tree, such as the bristlecone pine, decidedly exceed this. A tree was found in eastern Nevada that after felling showed 4,844 annual growth rings. Moreover, the cut was made 2.4 metres (8 feet) up from the ground so the tree's age must have been a bit more.[299]

Is it possible that a tree can live forever? The answer is no. But some can live for an exceedingly long time; possibly even until killed off by some cataclysmic climatic change, such as an ice age. The common or English yew apparently has the ability to renew itself from the original root. Trees have been observed flourishing within, and truly part of, the shell of the original tree, which may be quite viable though centuries old. It is no exaggeration to say that the yew tree at Fortingall, Scotland, is somewhere between 5,000 and 7,000 years old (see pages 60–61).

Table 1

Greatest Ages Attained by Different Species of Trees

First Thousand Years

Black cottonwood, *Populus trichocarpa*	c. 250
Bigleaf maple, *Acer macrophyllum*	c. 300
Grand fir, *Abies grandis*	c. 300
Silk cotton, *Ceiba pentandra*	> 300
Sugar maple, *Acer saccharum*	> 400
Mountain ash, *Eucalyptus regnans*	c. 500
Karri, *Eucalyptus diversicolor*	c. 500
Eastern white pine, *Pinus strobus*	c. 500
Red fir, *Abies magnifica*	c. 500
White fir, *Abies concolor*	c. 500
Port Orford cedar, *Chamaecyparis lawsoniana*	c. 600
Jeffrey pine, *Pinus jeffreyi*	600
Tulip tree, *Liriodendron tulipifera*	600
Western white pine, *Pinus monticola*	615
Engelmann spruce, *Picea engelmanni*	660
Noble fir, *Abies procera*	c. 700
Klinki pine, *Araucaria hunsteinii*	c. 700
Sugar pine, *Pinus lambertiana*	760
Giant jungle tree, *Shorea curtisii*	c. 800
Sitka spruce, *Picea sitchensis*	c. 900
Western larch, *Larix occidentalis*	915
Incense cedar, *Calocedrus decurrens*	< 1,000
Brazil-nut tree, *Bertholletia excelsa*	1,000
Pacific silver fir, *Abies amabilis*	c. 1,000
Himalayan cedar, *Cedrus deodara*	c. 1000

Second Thousand Years

English oak, *Quercus robur*	> 1,000
Ponderosa pine, *Pinus ponderosa*	1,047
Western hemlock, *Tsuga heterophylla*	1,238
Douglas-fir, *Pseudotsuga menziesii*	1,500
Western red cedar, *Thuja plicata*	c. 2,000
Olive, *Olea europaea*	c. 2,000
Kahikatea (white pine), *Dacrycarpus dacrydioides*	c. 2,000

Third Thousand Years

Yellow cedar, *Chamaecyparis nootkatensis*	c. 2,500
Coast redwood, *Sequoia sempervirens*	> 2,500
Sweet chestnut, *Castanea sativa*	> 2,500
Camphor tree, *Cinnamomum camphora*	c. 3,000
Montezuma baldcypress, *Taxodium mucronatum*	3,000
Western juniper, *Juniperus occidentalis*	c. 3,000
Taiwan cypress, *Chamaecyparis formosensis*	c. 3,000

Fourth Thousand Years

Oriental plane, *Platanus orientalis*	3,200
Huon pine, *Lagarostrobus franklinii*	3,460
Giant sequoia, *Sequoiadendron giganteum*	3,500
Alerce or Patagonian cypress, *Fitzroya cupressoides*	3,800
Kauri pine, *Agathis australis*	4,000
Baobab, *Adansonia digitata*	c. 4,000
Cryptomeria, *Cryptomeria japonica*	c. 4,000

Fifth Thousand Years

Bristlecone pine, *Pinus longaeva*	4,850

Sixth and Beyond Thousand Years

Common or English yew, *Taxus baccata*	> 5,000

Chart 1
World's Ten Tallest Trees Ever Measured

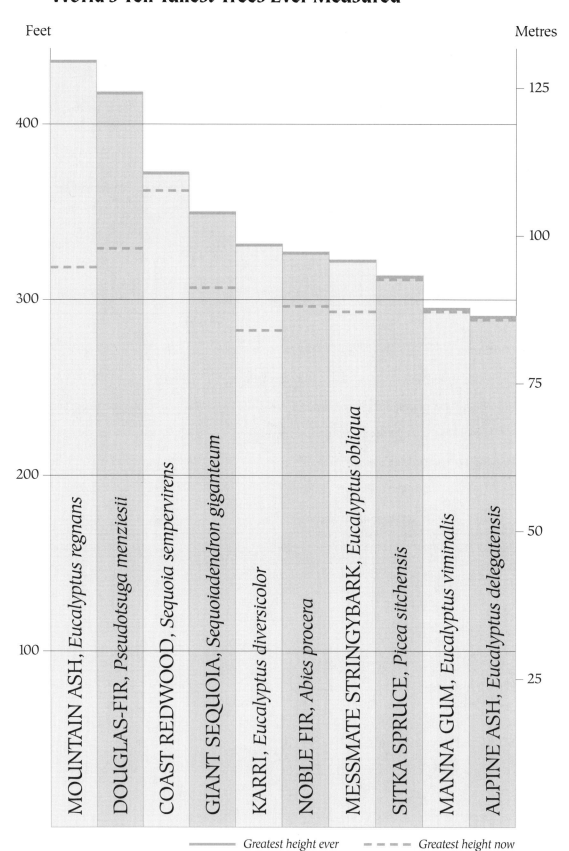

Feet

Metres

MOUNTAIN ASH, *Eucalyptus regnans*

DOUGLAS-FIR, *Pseudotsuga menziesii*

COAST REDWOOD, *Sequoia sempervirens*

GIANT SEQUOIA, *Sequoiadendron giganteum*

KARRI, *Eucalyptus diversicolor*

NOBLE FIR, *Abies procera*

MESSMATE STRINGYBARK, *Eucalyptus obliqua*

SITKA SPRUCE, *Picea sitchensis*

MANNA GUM, *Eucalyptus viminalis*

ALPINE ASH, *Eucalyptus delegatensis*

———— *Greatest height ever*   – – – – *Greatest height now*

Chart 2
Percent Tree Height Reduction from Forests in Pristine State to Modern Times

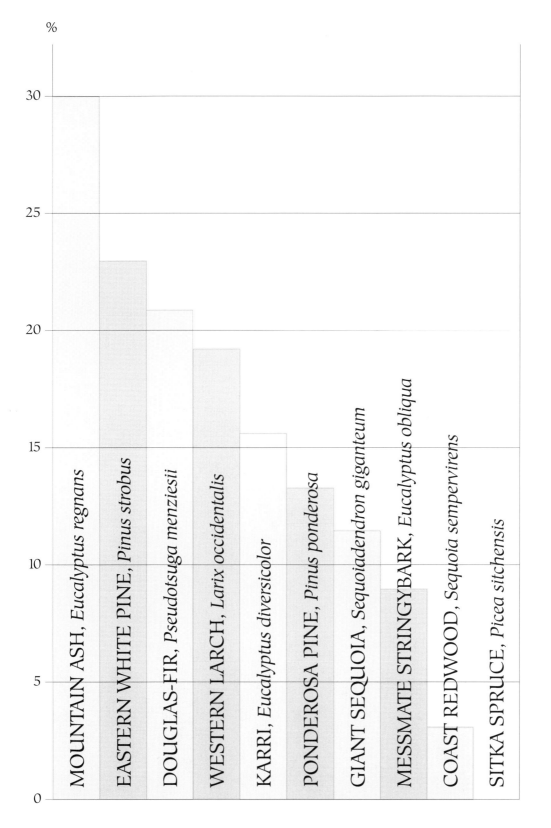

Chart 3
World's Ten Trees with Thickest Trunk Ever Measured

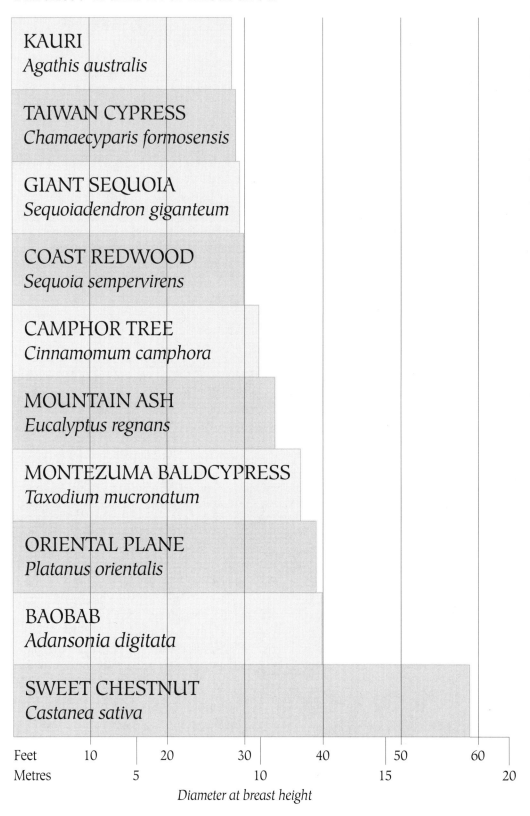

KAURI
Agathis australis

TAIWAN CYPRESS
Chamaecyparis formosensis

GIANT SEQUOIA
Sequoiadendron giganteum

COAST REDWOOD
Sequoia sempervirens

CAMPHOR TREE
Cinnamomum camphora

MOUNTAIN ASH
Eucalyptus regnans

MONTEZUMA BALDCYPRESS
Taxodium mucronatum

ORIENTAL PLANE
Platanus orientalis

BAOBAB
Adansonia digitata

SWEET CHESTNUT
Castanea sativa

| Feet | 10 | 20 | 30 | 40 | 50 | 60 |
| Metres | 5 | | 10 | | 15 | 20 |

Diameter at breast height

Chapter End Notes

PREFACE
1. Vancouver Archives, February 5, 1957.

REMARKABLE TREES OF BRITISH COLUMBIA AND THE PACIFIC NORTHWEST
2. Walter M. Draycott. "Early Days in Lynn Valley," the *North Shore Times*, North Vancouver, British Columbia, 1978, p. 29.
3. Walter M. Draycott. Personal correspondence to Ernest J. Beamish, December 2, 1951. In author's file.
4. Walter M. Draycott. Personal correspondence to Fred J. Clunk, February 10, 1960. In author's file.
5. John Parminter. "A Tale of a Tree," *Forest History Newsletter*, Forest History Association of British Columbia, January 1996. See also Francis Dickie. "Giants of British Columbian Forests," *Victoria Colonist*, Victoria, British Columbia, February 14, 1954, p. 9 (magazine section).
6. Walter M. Draycott. "Big Trees in British Columbia," Unpublished document, December 2, 1951. In author's file.
7. Anonymous. *Vancouver World*, Vancouver, British Columbia, October 3, 1906, p. 13.
8. Al Carder. *Forest Giants of the World, Past and Present*, Fitzhenry and Whiteside, Markham, Ontario, 1995, pp. 3, 4.
9. Ibid. p. 6.
10. Dave Bohn and Rodolfo Petsheck. *Kinsey Photographer*, Chronicle Books, San Francisco, 1982, pp. 151–153.
11. H.J. Elwes and A.H. Henry. *The Trees of Great Britain and Ireland*, R. and R. Clark Ltd., Edinburgh, 1909. Reprint 1970, vol. 4, p. 818. See also Al Carder. *Idem*, pp. 6, 11.
12. Robert Van Pelt. *Forest Giants of the Pacific Coast*, University of Washington Press, Seattle and London, 2001, p. 45.
13. Al Carder. *Idem*, pp. 8, 9, 11.
14. Ibid., p. 3.
15. Joan Hager. "Your Town and Mine," *Evergreen Monthly*, 11(2), March, 1947, p. 3. See also Byron Fish. "Largest Douglas Fir on Record Still Displays Its Defiance," *The Seattle Times*, June 23, 1954, p. 4.
16. Walter M. Draycott. *Lynn Valley: From the Wilds of Nature to Civilization*, North Shore Press, North Vancouver, British Columbia, 1919, p. 7.
17. H.J. Elwes and A.H. Henry. *Idem*, vol. 4, p. 818.
18. T.J. Starker. "Giant Growers of the Globe," *American Forests*, June 1935, pp. 266–68.
19. Robert Van Pelt. *Idem*, pp. 42, 43.
20. Robert Van Pelt. Ibid., pp. 42, 46.
21. Al Carder. *Idem*, p. 9.
22. Anne Kloppenborg, Alice Newinski, Eve Johnson. *Vancouver, A City Album*, Douglas and McIntyre, Vancouver/Toronto, 1991, p. xvii.
23. Robert Van Pelt. *Idem*, p. 17.
24. Al Carder. *Idem*, p, 32.
25. Al Carder. Ibid., pp. 73, 74.
26. Daniel Francis. *Encyclopedia of British Columbia*, Harbour Publishing, Madeira Park, British Columbia, 2000, p. 716.
27. Anonymous. *Dancing on a Cedar Stump*, Photo on title page, *Canadian Forestry Journal*, vol. XV, no. 11, Ottawa, November 1919. See also Fred Bodsworth, *The Illustrated Natural History of Canada: The Pacific Coast*, Natural Science of Canada, Toronto, 1970, p. 78.

28. Eric Nicol. *Vancouver, A City Album*, Doubleday, Toronto, 1970, p. 96. See also G.M. Lauridsen and A.A. Smith. *The Story of Port Angeles*, Lawman and Hanford Co., Seattle, 1937, opp. p. 81.

29. Robert Van Pelt. *Idem*, pp. 32, 33.

30. M.H.T. Fall. Personal correspondence, January 7, 1980. Mr. Fall enclosed in his letter a copy of a cruise tally card; the tree's highest point was measured from two locations.

31. Al Carder. *Idem*, p. 21. See also Van Pelt, *Idem*, p. 31.

32. Al Carder. Ibid., p. 21.

33. Robert Van Pelt. *Idem*, p. 37.

34. Robert Van Pelt. Ibid., pp. 30, 31, 34–36.

35. Al Carder. *Idem*, p. 20.

36. Robert Van Pelt. *Champion Trees of Washington State*, University of Washington Press, Seattle, Washington, 1996, pp. 15, 18.

37. Edmond P. Sheldon. *The Forest Wealth of Oregon*, State Printer, Salem, Oregon, 1904, p. 14 and frontispiece. See also H.J. Elwes and A.H. Henry. *Idem*, vol. 4, p. 818. Brian O'Brian. "On the Trail of the World's Largest Spruce," *Forest World*, Portland, Oregon, Summer 1988, pp. 22–33. Robert Van Pelt. *Idem*, 2001, p. 66.

38. Richard E. McArdle. "Some Notes on Maximum Sizes, Ages, and Yields of Forest Trees," Pacific Northwest Forest Experimental Station, Portland, Oregon, November 22, 1925. See also E.J. Hanzlik. *Trees and Forests of Western United States*, US Forest Service, Portland, Oregon, 1928, p. 76.

39. Anonymous. "Giants of Other Species," *ForesTalk Resource Magazine*, British Columbia Forest Service, Victoria, British Columbia, Spring 1978, p. 26.

40. Robert Van Pelt. *Idem*, 2001, p. 69.

41. Star Weiss. "Carmanah Valley," *Beautiful British Columbia* magazine, Victoria, British Columbia, Winter 1994, pp. 20, 21.

42. Robert Van Pelt. *Idem*, 1996, p. 19.

43. Bruce Obee. "Carmanah," *Beautiful British Columbia* magazine, Victoria, British Columbia, Winter, 1989, p. 5. See also Anonymous. "95-metre Spruce the World's Tallest?," *Times Colonist*, Victoria, British Columbia, June 11, 1988, p. A1. Steve Foster. Oregon City, Oregon. Personal correspondence. In author's file. S. Foster climbed the tree on October 16, 1992.

44. Ron Hildebrant. McKinleyville, California, Tall Trees Club Journal, Unpublished document, January 1998, p. 4. Also correspondence from him, November 8, 2000. In author's file. See also Robert Van Pelt, *Idem*, 2001, p. xxii.

45. Robert Van Pelt. *Idem*, 2001, p. 68.

46. Daniel Wood. "Hunting the Monster," *Westworld* magazine, September 2001, pp. 19–21.

47. Don Munday. "Ancients of the Sky Lines," *Illustrated Canadian Forests and Outdoors*, November 1931, pp. 25–27.

48. Robert Van Pelt. *Idem*, 2001, p. 89.

49. Ibid., p. 88

50. Robert Van Pelt. *Idem*, 1996, p. 3.

51. William M. Harlow and Ellwood S. Harrar. *Textbook of Dendrology*, 5th edition, McGraw-Hill, New York, 1950, p. 235. See also Irene O'Connor. *An Introduction to Quinault Valley Rain Forest*, Washingtonian Print, Hoquiam, Washington, 1962, p. 10. G.H. Collingwood and W.D. Brush. *Knowing Your Trees*, the American Forestry Association, Washington, DC, 1974, p. 161.

52. Joseph K. Henry. *Flora of Southern British Columbia and Vancouver Island*, W.J. Gage & Co. Ltd., Toronto, 1915, p. 101.

53. Robert Van Pelt. Personal correspondence, Seattle, Washington, December 10, 2003.

54. Arthur Lee Jacobson. *North American Landscape Trees*, Ten Speed Press, Berkeley, California, 1996, p. 313. See also Donald J. Leopold, William C. McCamb and Robert N. Miller. *Trees of the Central Hardwood Forests of North America*, Timber Press, Portland, Oregon, 1998, p. 237. There are anomalous instances of other broadleaf, temperate trees

reaching the 61-metre (200-foot) height. A 63.4-metre (208-foot) tanoak, *Lithocarpus densiflorus*, was found in northern California. The foliage of the ancient ginkgo tree, *Ginkgo biloba*, at Yongmon-san, South Korea, touches the 61-metre (200-foot) height.

55. H.A. Fowells, *Silvics of Forest Trees of the United States*, USDA Hdbk. 271, 1965, revised and approved 1975, p. 511. See also Anonymous. "Big Trees of British Columbia," *Register of Big Trees*, Government of British Columbia, 2003, p. 8.
56. Al Carder. *Idem*, p. 24.

OTHER REMARKABLE TREES OF THE WORLD

NORTH AMERICA

57. R.F. Scagel, et al. *An Evolutionary Survey of the Plant Kingdom*, Wadsworth Publishing, Belmont, California, 1965, pp. 498, 514. See also W.E. Willis, "Timber from Forest to Consumer," *Timber Trades Journal*, Ernest Benn Ltd., London, 1968, p. 141.
58. Al Carder. *Forest Giants of the World, Past and Present*. Fitzhenry and Whiteside, Markham, Ontario, 1995, p. 32.
59. Ron Hildebrant. "The Late Great Dyerville Giant Tree," McKinleyville, California, Unpublished document, 1993, p. 8. In author's file.
60. Ron Hildebrant and Michael Taylor. "Breaking News of November," Tall Trees Club Journal, McKinleyville, California, November 1997, p. 15. Unpublished document. In author's file.
61. Thomas Pakenham. *Remarkable Trees of the World*, Weidenfeld and Nicolson, London, 2002, p. 32. Also Robert Van Pelt, Personal correspondence, Seattle, Washington, December 10, 2003.
62. Robert Van Pelt. *Forest Giants of the Pacific Coast*, University of Washington Press, Seattle and London, 2001, p. 17.
63. Ibid., p. 22.
64. H.J. Elwes and A.H. Henry. *The Trees of Great Britain and Ireland*, R. and R. Clark, Ltd., Edinburgh, 1909, Reprint 1970, vol. 3, p. 692.
65. S.J. Record and R.W. Hess. *Timbers of the New World*, Yale University Press, London, 1943, p. 28. See also F.C. Lane, *The Story of Trees*, Doubleday and Co., Garden City, New York, 1952, p. 58.
66. Ron Hildebrant and Michael Taylor. *Idem*, February, 1998, p. 8.
67. Walter Fry and John R. White. *Big Trees*, Stanford University Press, California, 1930, p. 51. See also Edwin A. Menninger. *Fantastic Trees*, Viking Press, New York, 1967, p. 195.
68. Jack McCormick. *The Living Forest*, Harper and Brothers, New York, 1959, p. 86. See also Jeremy Joan Hewes. *Redwoods: The World's Largest Trees*, Rand McNally and Co., London, 1981, p. 101.
69. Robert Van Pelt. *Idem*, p. 2.
70. Ibid., p. 8.
71. Ibid., p. 4.
72. Wendell D. Flint. *To Find the Biggest Tree*, Sequoia Natural History Association, Three Rivers, California, 1987, pp. 84, 92.
73. Ron Hildebrant. "The Maple Creek Tree: Setting the Record Straight for its Volume," Unpublished Statement, 1993, p. 10. In author's file. See also Robert Van Pelt. *Idem*, p. 16.
74. Jeremy Joan Hewes. *Idem*, pp. 61, 62.
75. Stephen F. Arno and Ramona P. Hammerly. *Northwest Trees*, The Mountaineers, Seattle, 1977, p. 106.
76. Robert Van Pelt. *Idem*, p. 94.
77. Robert Van Pelt. *Champion Trees of Washington State*, University of Washington Press, Seattle, 1996, p. 8. See also David More and John White. *The Illustrated Encyclopedia of Trees*, Timber Press, Portland, Oregon, 2002, pp. 144, 145.
78. Robert Van Pelt. *Idem*, 2001, p. 96.

79. Donald Culross Peattie. *A Natural History of Western Trees*, Bonanza Books, New York, 1973, pp. 19–22.
80. Frank T. Callahan. Personal correspondence, Central Point, Oregon, December 25, 1997 and February 8, 1998. In author's file.
81. Robert Van Pelt. *Idem*, 2001, pp. 76, 79.
82. Henry Clapper. "An Aged Sugar Pine," *American Forests* magazine, March 1982, p. 14.
83. Robert Van Pelt. *Idem*, 2001, p. 117.
84. Ibid.
85. Anonymous. "Big Trees of British Columbia," Ministry of Environment, Land and Parks, *Big Tree Register*, March, 2001, p. 7.
86. W.M. Harlow and E.S. Harrar. *Textbook of Dendrology*, 5th Ed., McGraw-Hill, New York, 1969, p. 99.
87. Robert Van Pelt. Personal correspondence, Seattle, Washington, December 10, 2003. In author's file.
88. Alan Mitchell. *A Field Guide to the Trees of Britain and Northern Europe*, Collins, London, 1974, p. 157.
89. H.J. Elwes and A.H. Henry. *Idem*, vol. 5, p. 35. See also Charles S. Sargent. *The Silva of North America*, Peter Smith, New York, 1897, vol. XI, p. 12.
90. H.A. Fowells. *Silvics of Forest Trees of the United States*, USDA Hdbk. 271, 1965, revised and approved 1975, p. 332.
91. Ibid. See also Scott Leathart. *Whence Our Trees*, Foulsham, London, 1991, p. 133, and Deborah S. Johnson. Asssistant Editor, American Forestry Assoc., Washington, DC, Personal correspondence, November 10, 1983. In author's file.
92. Robert Van Pelt. *Idem*, 2001, p. 144.
93. Ibid.
94. Ibid., p. 146.
95. Whit Bronaugh. "In Search of Old-growth Giants," *American Forests*, Spring 2000, p. 46. See also Van Pelt. *Idem*, 2001, p. 144.
96. H.A. Fowells. *Idem*, p. 483.
97. Frank T. Callahan. "The Word for the World Is Conifer," *Mountains and Rivers*, Quarterly Journal of Natural History of the Klamath-Siskiyou Region, vol. 1 no.1, Fall 2000, p. 13.
98. Robert Van Pelt. *Idem* 2001, p. 102. Also personal correspondence from him, Seattle, Washington, December 10, 2003. In author's file.
99. Charles Sprague Sargent. *Manual of the Trees of North America*, vol. 1, Dover Publications, New York, 1965, p. 352.
100. Donald J. Leopold, William C. McComb, Robert N. Muller. *Trees of the Central Hardwood Forests of North America*. Timber Press, Portland, Oregon, 1998, p. 240.
101. Robert Van Pelt. Personal correspondence, Seattle, Washington, December 10, 2003. In author's file.
102. Joseph Kaye Henry. *Flora of Southern British Columbia and Vancouver Island*, W.J. Cage & Co. Ltd., Toronto, 1915, p. 101.
103. Arthur Lee Jacobson. *Idem*, p. 313.
104. Audrey Grescoe and Bob Herger. *Giants: The Colossal Trees of Pacific North America*, Raincoast Books, Vancouver, 1997, p. 90.
105. Arthur Lee Jacobson. *Idem*, p. 313.
106. Al Carder. *Idem*, p. 47.
107. Victor Jimenez. *El Arbol de el Tule en Las Historia*, codex Editores, Mexico, 1990, pp. 96, 97. Jimenez' book has been translated into English by N.P. Videla, see p. 90 of translation. The trunk of the Tule Tree is roughly oval in outline being about 7.6 metres (25 feet) across one way and 12.2 metres (40 feet) in the opposite direction. The 11.6-metre (38-foot) diameter measurement was determined by placing a rope around the tree at a man's chest height, pulling it tight and calculating the diameter from the perimeter. A copy of the translation is in author's file.
108. Ibid., p. 4. Translation p. 6.

109. Ibid., pp. 7, 8. Translation pp. 10, 11.

110. Ibid. pp. 16, 17. Translation pp. 19–22.

111. W.C. Hall et al. "Genetic Uniformity of El Arbol del Tule," *Madrono*, vol. 37, 1990, p. 1. See also Thomas Pakenham. *Idem*, p. 28.

112. Victor Jimenez. *Idem*, p. 72. Translation p. 83. See also Al Carder, *Idem*, p. 55.

EUROPE

113. Owen Johnson. *Champion Trees of Britain and Ireland, The Tree Register,* Whiffel Books, Stowmarket, Suffolk, England, 2003, p. 91. See also Alan Mitchell. *Alan Mitchell's Trees of Britain*, Harper Collins, London, 1996, p. 313 and Jon Stokes and Donald Rodger, *The Heritage Trees of Britain and Northern Ireland*, Constable, London, 2004, p. 84.

114. Thomas Pakenham. *Meetings With Remarkable Trees*, Weidenfeld and Nicolson, London, 1996, p. 19. See also Owen Johnson. Ibid.

115. Al Carder. *Forest Giants of the World, Past and Present*, Fitzhenry and Whiteside, Markham, Ontario, 1995, p. 92. See also Jon Stokes and Donald Rodger, *Idem*, p. 87.

116. Andrew Morton. *Tree Heritage of Britain and Ireland*, Swan Hill Press, Shrewsbury, England, 1998, p. 98.

117. J.H. Wilks. *Trees of the British Isles in History and Legend*. Frederick Muller, London, 1972, pp. 198, 199.

118. Al Carder. *Idem*, p. 92.

119. H.J. Elwes and A.H. Henry. *The Trees of Great Britain and Ireland*, R. and R. Clark, Edinburgh, 1909, vol. 2, p. 331.

120. Owen Johnson. *The Sussex Tree Book*, Pomegranate Press, Westmeston, Sussex, 1998, p. 42. See also Jon Stokes and Donald Rodger, *Idem*, p. 123.

121. Andrew Morton. *The Trees of Shropshire*, Airlife, Shrewsbury, England, 1986, pp. 42, 43.

122. J.H. Wilks. *Idem*, pp. 198, 199.

123. Anna Lewington and Edward Parker. *Ancient Trees, Trees that Live for a Thousand Years*, Collins and Brown, London, 1999, p. 86.

124. Robert Boudu and Michel Viard. *Abres Souverains*, Éditons de May, Paris, 1988, pp. 82, 83.

125. Al Carder. *Idem*, p. 96.

126. Anna Lewington and Edward Parker. *Idem*, p. 87.

127. Thomas Pakenham. *Remarkable Trees of the World*, Weidenfeld and Nicolson, London, 2002, p. 78.

128. Anna Lewington and Edward Parker. *Idem*, pp. 77, 87.

129. Al Carder. *Idem*, p. 98.

130. Ibid.

131. F.A. Pouchet. *The Universe: Or the Infinitely Great and the Infinitely Little*, Blackie and Son, London, 1868, p. 375.

132. Scott Leathart. *Whence Our Trees?* Foulsham, Slough, England, 1991, p. 170. See also Al Carder. *Idem*, p. 113.

133. Harry D. Tiemann. "What are the Largest Trees in the World?," *Journal of Forestry*, July 1935, pp. 910, 911.

134. Luigi Scaccabarozzi. Milan, Italy, Personal correspondence, December 7, 1988, March 31, 1990. In author's file.

135. Hugh Johnson. *The International Book of Trees*, Simon and Schuster, New York, 1973, p. 163.

136. Al Carder. *Idem*, p. 114.

137. Luigi Scaccabarozzi. Milan, Italy, Personal correspondence, October 25, 1998. In author's file.

138. Al Carder. *Idem*, pp. 114, 115.

139. Scott Leathart. *Idem*, p. 170. See also personal correspondence from Riva Giovanni, Caronno Pertusella, Italy, February 6, 1992. In author's file.

140. Alan Mitchell. *Idem*, p. 210. See also Andrew Morton. *Idem*, pp. 95–97. Thomas

Pakenham. *Idem*, pp. 168, 169.

141. P.H.B. Gardner. "The Tortworth Chestnut," *Quarterly Journal of Forestry*, July 1961, p. 291. See also Owen Johnson. *Idem*, 2003, p. 42.

142. Owen Johnson. Ibid.

143. Andrew Morton. *Idem*, pp. 167, 168. See also Anna Lewington and Edward Parker. *Idem*, p. 71. Archie Miles. *Silva, The Tree in Britain*, Ebury Press, London, 1999, pp. 163, 166.

144. J. Edward Milner. *The Tree Book*, Collins and Brown, London, 1992, p. 84. See also Archie Miles. *Idem*, p. 166. Jane Gifford. *The Wisdom of Trees*, Sterling Publishing Co., Toronto, Ontario, 2001, p. 136.

145. Archie Miles. *Idem*, pp. 169–171. See also Owen Johnson. *Idem*, 2003, p. 104.

146. John Lowe. *The Yew Trees of Great Britain and Ireland*, MacMillan & Co., London, 1897, pp. 85, 191. See also Hans Molisch. *The Longevity of Plants*, E.W. Fulling, New York, 1938, p. 46. Hal Hartzell. *The Yew Tree, A Thousand Whispers*, Hulogosi Press, Eugene, Oregon, 1991, p. 5.

147. J.H. Fabre. *The Wonder Book of Plant Life*, T. Fisher Unwin, London, p. 26. See also Owen Johnson. *Idem*, 2003, p. 104.

148. Archie Miles. *Idem*, pp. 169–171.

149. Anna Lewington and Edward Parker. *Idem*, p. 71. See also Archie Miles, *Idem*, p. 166.

150. J.H. Wilks. *Idem*, p. 102. See also Trevor Baxter. *The Eternal Yew*, Self Publishing Association, Hanley Swan, Worcestershire, 1922, pp. 142, 143. Anand Chetan and Diana Brueton. *The Sacred Yew*, Arkana, London, 1994, pp. xi, 8, 25. Andrew Morton. *Idem*, p. 103. Richard Maybe. *Flora Britannica*, Chatto & Winders, London, 1998, p. 193. Anna Lewington and Edward Parker. *Idem*, p. 71.

151. Alan Mitchell. *Idem*, p. 155.

152. Anand Chetan and Diana Brueton. *Idem*, pp. 39, 256.

153. Cindy Stevens. *Yew*, Sage Press, Rye, East Sussex, England, 1999, p. 12.

154. Trevor Baxter. *Idem*, pp. 26, 27.

155. Al Carder. *Idem*, p. 111.

156. Thomas Pakenham. *Idem*, p. 98.

157. Hans Molisch. *Idem*, p. 64. See also F.A. Pouchet. *Idem*, pp. 371, 372.

158. A.J. King. "Some Trees of Interest in the 1840s," *Quarterly Journal of Forestry*, The Royal Forestry Society, January 1959, p. 55.

159. Arthur Lee Jacobson. *North American Landscape Trees*, Ten Speed Press, Berkeley, California, 1996, p. 464.

160. H.J. Elwes and A.H. Henry. *Idem*, p. 623.

161. Jean Dupuis. *Marvellous World of Trees*, Abbey Library, London, 1976, p. 12.

162. B.K. Boom and H. Kleijn. *The Glory of the Tree*, George G. Harrop & Co., London, 1966, p. 70. See also John Evelyn. *Silva: or a Discourse of Forest Trees*, J. Todd, York, England, 1786, vol. II, p. 181. Russel Meiggs. *Trees and Timber in the Ancient Mediterranean World*, Clarendon Press, Oxford, 1922, p. 27.

163. Richard St. Barbe Baker. *Famous Trees of Bible Lands*, H.H. Creaves Ltd., London, 1974, p. 47.

SOUTHERN HEMISPHERE

164. Anna Lewington and Edward Parker. *Ancient Trees, Trees that Live for a Thousand Years*, Collins and Brown, London, 1999, p. 135.

165. John Halkett and E.V. Sale. *The World of the Kauri*, Reed Methuen, Auckland, 1986, pp. 6, 7.

166. Al Carder. *Forest Giants of the World, Past and Present*, Fitzhenry and Whiteside, Markham, Ontario, 1995, pp. 57, 58.

167. Ibid.

168. John Halkett and E.V. Sale. *Idem*, p. 170.

169. J.T. Salmon. *The Native Trees of New Zealand*, A.H. and A.W. Reed, Wellington, 1980,

pp. 44, 98.

170. Paul Hamlyn. *New Zealand Trees, Conifers*, Collins, Auckland, 1979, p. 41. See also J.T. Salmon. *Idem*, p. 51.

171. S.W. Burstall and E.V. Sale. *Great Trees of New Zealand*, A.H. and A.W. Reed, Wellington, 1984, p. 1.

172. J.T. Salmon. *Idem*, p. 40.

173. R.F. Scagel, et al. *An Evolutionary Survey of the Plant Kingdom*, Wadsworth Publishing Co. Inc., Belmont, California, 1965, pp. 498, 514. See also W.E. Willis. *Timber from Forest to Consumer*, Published for *Timber Trades Journal*, Ernest Denn Ltd., London, 1968, p. 141.

174. Ken J. Simpfendorfer. "Big Trees in Victoria," unpublished treatise, 49 pp., 1983. Ken Simpfendorfer died before this could be published. The quote is on p. 23. Document in author's files.

175. Ibid., p. 22.

176. Colin Silcock. "Tree Giants of Gippsland," *Gippsland Heritage Journal*, March 1996, pp. 35, 36.

177. Ken Simpfendorfer. *Idem*, pp. 2, 12. See also Michael Jones. *Prolific in God's Gifts*, George Allen & Unwin, Sydney, 1983, p. 80.

178. Thomas Pakenham. *Remarkable Trees of the World*, Weidenfeld & Nicolson, London, 2002, p. 168.

179. Ken Simpfendorfer. *Idem*, p. 23.

180. Al Carder. *Idem*, p. 69.

181. Ibid., p. 75.

182. Ibid., pp. 70, 71.

183. Ken Simpfendorfer. *Idem*, p. 36.

184. Ibid., pp. 26, 27.

185. Bernard Mace. "Mueller—Champion of Victoria's Giant Trees," *The Victorian Naturalist*, vol. 113(4), 1996, p. 206.

186. Al Carder. *Idem*, pp. 70, 72. See also Bernard Mace. *Idem*, p. 204. J.E. Hickey, P. Kostoglou, G.J. Sargison. "Tasmania's Tallest Trees," *Tasforests*, vol. 12, December 2000, p. 105.

187. Edward Kynaston. *A Man on Edge*, Allen Lane, London, 1981, pp. 280–292.

188. William Macready. "The Big Tree of Victoria," *Argus* newspaper, Melbourne, May 28, 1899, p. 14.

189. Ken J. Simpfendorfer. *Idem*, pp. 4–6.

190. Paul Roberts. Pakenham, Victoria, Australia. Personal correspondence, April 24, June 12, July 17, August 22, and October 22, 2002. P. Roberts has travelled over the states of Victoria and Tasmania studying giant trees and recording their history.

191. Al Carder. *Idem*, pp. 70, 72.

192. N.J. Caire. "Notes on the Giant Trees of Victoria," *The Victorian Naturalist* 21, 1905, p. 124.

193. Al Carder. *Idem*, pp. 76, 77.

194. A.D. Helms. "A Giant Eucalypt," *Australian Forestry*, vol. 9, 1945, pp. 25–28.

195. Al Carder. *Idem*, p. 81. Also see Robert Van Pelt. Personal correspondence, Seattle, Washington, December 10, 2003. In author's file.

196. Ibid. Al Carder.

197. D.E. Hutchins. *Australian Forestry*, Government Printer, Perth, 1916, pp. 84, 85.

198. Ibid.

199. Al Carder. *Idem*, p. 82.

200. Ibid.

201. Robert Van Pelt. Personal communication, Seattle, Washington, December 10, 2003.

202. H.D. Tiemann. "What are the Largest Trees in the World?," *Journal of Forestry*, July 1935, pp. 905, 906.

203. Al Carder. *Idem*, p. 80. See also Tiemann. Ibid., p. 906.

204. Boland et al. *Idem*, pp. 306, 450, 470. See also J.E. Hickey, P. Kostoglou, and G.J.

Sargison. *Idem*, p. 105.

205. H.J. Elwes and A.H. Henry. *The Trees of Great Britain and Ireland*, R. and R. Clark, Edinburgh, 1909, vol. VI, p. 1456. See also T.H. Everett. *Living Trees of the World*, Doubleday, New York, 1968, p. 37. Martin Chudnoff. *Tropical Timbers of the World*, Forest Products Laboratory, Forest Service, USDA, 1979, p. 145. Mitchell Beazley. *The International Book of the Forest*, Simon and Schuster, New York, 1981, p. 68. Anthony Boadle. "Conservationists Save Ancient Rainforest," *Times Colonist* newspaper, Victoria, BC, April 3, 1991, p. A5 quotes a report from Santiago, Chile. Al Carder. *Idem*, pp. 161–2. Anna Lewington. *Atlas of the Rain Forests*, Raintree Steck-Vaughn, Austin, Texas, 1997, pp. 44, 45. Robert Van Pelt. Personal communication, Seattle, Washington, December 10, 2003.

TROPICS

206. T.C. Whitmore. *An Introduction to Tropical Rain Forests*, Clarendon Press, Oxford, 1992, p. 7. See also John Terborgh. *Diversity and the Tropical Rain Forest*, Scientific American Library, New York, 1992, p. 126.

207. John Terborgh. Ibid., p. 9.

208. Nathaniel Altman. *Sacred Trees*, Sierra Club, San Francisco, 1994, p. 26.

209. T.C. Whitmore. *Idem*, p. 50.

210. Al Carder. *Forest Giants of the World, Past and Present*, Fitzhenry and Whiteside, Markham, Ontario, 1995, pp. 139, 140.

211. A.G. Voorhoeve. *Liberian High Forest Trees*, Wageningen, Netherlands, 1965, p. 69.

212. Thomas Pakenham. *The Remarkable Baobab*, Weidenfeld & Nicolson, London, 2004, pp. 87–93.

213. Keith Coates Palgrave. *Trees of Southern Africa*, Struik Publishers, Cape Town, 1988, pp. 587, 588. See also Piet van Wyk. *Field Guide to the Trees of the Kruger National Park*, Struik Publishers, Cape Town, 1984, p. 159.

214. Keith Coates Palgrave. Ibid.

215. Keith Coates Palgrave. Ibid. See also Thomas Pakenham. *Remarkable Trees of the World*, Weidenfeld & Nicolson, London, 2002, p. 19.

216. Vincent Serventy. *Australian Native Trees*, Reed Books Ltd., Sydney, 1984, p. 121.

217. Al Carder. *Idem*, pp. 140, 141.

218. Edward Ayensu. *Jungles*, Crown Publishers, New York, 1980, p. 179.

219. Anna Lewington and Edward Parker. *Ancient Trees, Trees that Live for a Thousand Years*, Collins and Brown, London, 1999, p. 140.

220. P.W. Richards. *The Tropical Rain Forest*, Second Edition, Cambridge University Press, London, 1996, p. 4.

221. S. Dillon Ripley. *The Land and Wildlife of Tropical Asia*, Time Incorporated, New York, 1964, p. 53. See also Gerald Cubitt and Junaidi Payne. *Wild Malaysia*, New Holland Publishers, London, 1990, p. 26.

222. T.C. Whitmore. *Tropical Rain Forest of the Far East*, Clarendon Press, Oxford, 1975, p. 175.

223. Steve Yates and Terry Domico. *The Nature of Borneo*, Facts on File, New York, 1992, p. 83. See also Al Carder. *Idem*, pp. 141, 142. James H. Flynn, Jr. and Charles D. Holder. *A Guide to Useful Woods of the World*, Forest Products Soc., Madison, Wisconsin, 2001, p. 212.

224. Yates and Domico. Ibid.

225. T.C. Whitmore. *Idem*, pp. 175, 176. See also S.B. Collard III. *Green Giants*, NorthWord Press, Minocqua, Wisconsin, 1994, p. 22.

226. Ibid. T.C. Whitmore, p. 175. See also K. Paijmans. *New Guinea Vegetation*, Elsevier Scientific Publishing Co., Amsterdam, Oxford, New York, 1976, p. 63.

227. P.W. Richards. *The Tropical Rainforest*, Cambridge University Press, London, 1972, p. 4. See also K.A. Longman and J. Jenik. *Tropical Forest and Its Environment*, 2nd Edition, Harlow, Essex, England, 1987, p. 159. Anna Lewington. *Atlas of the Rainforest*, Steck-

Vaughn, Austin, Texas, pp. 38, 39.

228. Sandra Holmes. *Trees of the World*, Bantam Books, Toronto, 1974, p. 87.

229. T.C. Whitmore. *Idem*, p. 74.

230. Art Wolfe and Sir Ghillean Prance. *Rainforests of the World*, Crown Publishers, New York, 1998, p. 94.

231. T.H. Everett. *Living Trees of the World*, Doubleday, New York, 1968, p. 74. See also Lorus and Margery Milne. *Living Plants of the World*, Random House, New York, 1975, pp. 283, 284. Cameron Young. "Once Waxed Tall," *ForesTalk Resource Magazine*, Summer 1980, British Columbia Ministry of Forests, p. 18.

232. David L. Jones. *Palms Throughout the World*, Smithsonian Institution Press, Washington, DC, 1995, p. 291.

ASIA

233. Zhao Ji, Zheng Guangmei, Won Huadon, and Xu Jialin. *The Natural History of China*, Collins, London, 1990, pp. 65, 139.

234. Al Carder. *Forest Giants of the World, Past and Present*, Fitzhenry and Whiteside, Markham, Ontario, 1995, pp. 132, 133.

235. Keith Rushforth. *Conifers*, Facts on File Publications, Oxford, England, 1987, pp. 202, 203. See also Arthur Lee Jacobson. *North American Landscape Trees*, Ten Speed Press, Berkeley, California, 1996, p. 613.

236. Arthur Lee Jacobson. Ibid.

237. Janet M. Poor. *Plants that Merit Attention: Trees*, Timber Press, Portland, Oregon, 1984, c. pp. 83, 84. See also Scott Leathart. *Whence Our Trees*, Foulsham, London, 1991, pp. 97–100. Arthur Lee Jacobson. *Idem*, p. 105.

238. Scott Leathart. *Idem*, p. 99. Al Carder. *Idem*, pp. 128, 129.

239. Gisele Ono. Personal correspondence, March 25, 1996, October 14, and December 7, 2002. In author's file.

240. Thomas Pakenham. *Remarkable Trees of the World*, Weidenfeld & Nicolson, London, 2002, pp. 104–107.

241. Arthur Lee Jacobson. *Idem*, p. 117.

242. H.J. Elwes and A.H. Henry. *The Trees of Great Britain and Ireland*, R. and R. Clark, Edinburgh, 1909, vol. 5, p. 1150.

243. Yoshida Shigeruand Kanie Setsuko. *Remaining Big Trees on Mother Earth*, Tokyo, Kodansha, 2002.

TREES OF LESSER STATURE, BRITISH COLUMBIA

244. Robert Van Pelt. *Forest Giants of the Pacific Coast*, University of Washington Press, Seattle and London, 2001, p. 128.

245. Randy Stoltmann. *Guide to the Record Trees of British Columbia*, Western Canada Wilderness Committee, 1993, p. 31.

246. Robert Van Pelt. *Idem*, pp. 69, 122.

247. Anonymous. Western Canada Wilderness Committee, Educational Report, vol. 15, no. 1, Winter Spring 1996, Vancouver, BC, p. 2.

248. Charles S. Sargent. *Manual of the Trees of North America*, vol. 1 of two vol., Dover Publications, New York, 1965, p. 55.

249. Robert Van Pelt. *Idem*, p. 158.

250. Arthur Lee Jacobson. *North American Landscape Trees*, Ten Speed Press, Berkeley, California, 1996, p. 5.

251. Roberta Parish. *Tree Book: Learning to Recognize Trees of British Columbia*, Canadian Forest Service, Victoria, BC, 1994, p. 77. See also Reese Halter and Nancy J. Turner. *Native Trees of British Columbia*, Global Forest Society, 2003, p. 59.

252. Robert Van Pelt. *Idem*, p. 156.

253. Ibid., p. 164.

254. Ibid., p. 168.

255. Robert Van Pelt. Personal communication, Seattle, Washington, December 10, 2003.

256. H.A. Fowells. *Silvics of Forest Tress of the United States*, Agric. Hdbk. 271, USDA Forest Service, Washington, DC, 1975, p. 238. See also James H. Flynn, Jr. and Charles D. Holder. *A Guide to Useful Woods of the World*, Forest Products Soc., Madison, Wisconsin, 2001, p. 318.

257. Robert Van Pelt. Personal communication, Seattle, Washington, December 10, 2003.

258. William M. Harlow and Ellwood S. Harrar. *Textbook of Dendrology*, McGraw-Hill, New York, 1958, p. 117.

259. H.J. Elwes and A.H. Henry. *The Trees of Great Britain and Ireland*, R. and R. Clark Ltd., Edinburgh, 1909, reprint 1970, vol. 2, p. 401.

260. Arthur Lee Jacobson. *Idem*, p. 22.

261. Robert Van Pelt. *Idem*, p. 13.

262. D.M. van Gelderen et al. *Maples of the World*, Timber Press, Portland, Oregon, 1994, pp. 19, 180.

263. Arthur Lee Jacobson. *Idem*, pp. 46, 47. See also Owen Johnson. *Champion Trees of Britain and Ireland*, The Tree Register, Whiffel Books, Suffolk, England, 2003, p. 33.

264. H.A. Fowells. *Idem*, p. 52.

265. D.M. van Gelderen et al. *Idem*, pp. 179, 180.

266. R.M. Burns and B.H. Honkala. *Silvics of North America*, vol. 2, Hardwoods, Agric. Hdbk. 654, Forest Service, Washington, D.C., 1990, p. 83.

OTHER TREES OF LESSER STATURE, THE WORLD

267. Arthur Lee Jacobson. *North American Landscape Trees*, Ten Speed Press, Berkeley, California, 1996, p. 93. See also Frank T. Callahan. "The Word For the World is Conifer," *Mountains and Rivers*, Quarterly Journal of Natural History of the Klamath-Siskiyou Region, Fall 2000, p. 13.

268. Robert Van Pelt. *Forest Giants of the Pacific Coast*, University of Washington Press, Seattle and London, 2001, p. 82.

269. Al Carder. *Forest Giants of the World, Past and Present*, Fitzhenry and Whiteside, Markham, Ontario, 1995, p. 43.

270. Robert Van Pelt. *Idem*, pp. 107, 115, 183.

271. Ibid., pp. 113, 183.

272. H.A. Fowells. *Silvics of Forest Trees of the United States*, Agric. Hdbk. No. 271, USDA Washington, DC, 1965, p. 358.

273. Robert Van Pelt. *Idem*, pp. 108, 183.

274. H.A. Fowells. *Idem*, p. 358.

275. Robert Van Pelt. *Idem*, p. 132.

276. Ibid., p. 136.

277. Arthur Lee Jacobson. *Idem*, p. 7.

278. Alan Mitchell and David More. *The Guide to Trees of Canada and North America*, Dragon's World, Limpsfield, Surrey, England, 1987, p. 150.

279. Robert Van Pelt. *Champion Trees of Washington State*, University of Washington Press, Seattle, 1996, p. 17.

280. Robert Van Pelt. *Idem*, 2001, p. 173.

281. Ibid., p. 177.

282. William M. Harlow and Ellwood S. Harrar. *Textbook of Dendrology*, 5th Edition, McGraw-Hill, New York, 1968, p. 134.

283. Keith Rushforth. *Conifers*, Facts on File Publications, Oxford, England, 1987, p. 152.

284. Philip Henry Gosse. *The Romances of Natural History*, Lippincott, Philadelphia, 1875, pp. 136, 137. See also Royal Dixon and Franklyn E. Fitch. *The Human Side of Trees* (*Wonders of the Tree World*), Frederick A. Stokes, New York, 1917, p. 143.

285. Russell M. Burns and Barbara H. Honkala. *Silvics of North America*, vol. 2, Hardwoods, Agric. Hdbk. 654, Forest Service, USDA, Washington, DC, 1990, pp. 507–509.

286. Alan Mitchell. *Alan Mitchell's Trees of Great Britain*, Harper Collins, London, 1996, p.

316.

287. John Evelyn. *Silva: or a Discourse of Forest Trees*, J. Todd, York, vol. II, 1786, p. 198.

288. Thomas Pakenham. *Meetings With Remarkable Trees*, Weidenfeld & Nicolson, London, 1996, p. 27.

289. Al Carder. *Idem*, p. 53.

290. Victor Jimenez. *El Arbol de El Tule en la Historia*, Codex, Tule, 1990, p. 98. (English translation by Nancy Plankey Videla, in author's file).

291. Al Carder. *Idem*, p. 113.

292. Al Carder. *Idem*, pp. 148, 149.

293. J.H. Wilks. *Trees of the British Isles in History and Legend*, Frederick Muller, London, 1972, p. 75. See also Andrew Morton. *Tree Heritage of Britain and Ireland*, Swan Hill Press, Shrewsbury, England, 1998, pp. 153, 155.

294. John M. Haller. "The Giant Ceiba of Palin," *American Forests*, December 1985, pp. 48–50, 62, 63.

295. Robert Van Pelt. Personal correspondence, Seattle, Washington, December 10, 2003. In author's file.

296. Andrew Morton. *Idem*, p. 47.

297. Michael J. Shields. Personal correspondence, July 5, 1994. In author's file.

298. David L. Jones. *Palms Throughout the World*, Smithsonian Institution Press, Washington DC, 1995, p. 234.

THE TALLEST, LARGEST AND OLDEST TREES

299. Jane Braxton Little. "Time Line," *American Forests*, Winter 2004, pp. 22–27.

Index